The Three Year Pond
and Other Absurdities

Simon Pollard

Dedication

I dedicate this book to my son, Ross, who was inadvertently a major part of this story. He was a boy at the start of it and is now (mostly) a very mature teenager growing into manhood. Thanks mate!

To Al,

Put simply, it's all about responsibility.

Best wishes, enjoy!

Simon

Foreword

I first met Simon Pollard when he managed to clear my very weed encrusted brick path, which he did efficiently, cheerfully and at a very reasonable price. I soon came to realise that he was capable of much, much more and over the years he carried out various jobs around my windmill. Then, we moved to a Victorian town house which had been sorely neglected by its previous occupant. Here, Simon came into his own. Could he do shelving? He certainly could and made and installed beautiful bookshelves from floor to ceiling in the dining room, to be used as a library, and in my and my wife's offices. How about spindles for the staircase? No problem. And cupboards in the bedrooms? Easy, and after ten years without a single warp, unlike those of the awful Sharon, about whom you will read in this book. Over the years I have seen Simon metamorphose from a teacher who had enough of feral brats to a journeying handyman, to a Handyman for All Seasons and now to A Simple Life. You can read this book as the story of one man's search to find himself, or to find happiness, or as a love story or as a manual on garden design, or as just a rollicking good read which treats disaster and triumph in very much the same way. It is, like its author, a compellingly honest book, which has useful pointers in how to avoid being taken in by deceitful clients or smart-talking purveyors of snake oil. I'm not entirely convinced by Simon's 'Law of Attraction', but it has certainly worked for him, and after all, anyone who can get a teenage son to talk to him, never mind accompany him on week-long walks, has to be getting something right. This is a lovely book and I wish Simon and his new wife and his book and his business every success – they deserve it.

Gordon Corrigan

Disclaimer

This is a book about me, and it's about my thoughts and thinking. If you've been part of my life and you're in it, I hope you're honoured. If not I'm sorry I have no desire to upset anyone, these are my thoughts and interpretations. I have changed the names of some people I know might find my comments contentious. That's it.

Who ever you are, I look forward to reading your book.

Acknowledgements

Firstly obviously, Gillian. She is my wife and best friend, she slows me down and speeds me up, curbs my excesses and pushes me beyond my comfort zones and never stops boxing clever in my corner. She also helped out with editing, wrote the blurb and sussed out how to make the pictures in this book easy to make and produce. Thank you Gorgeous.

And Wendy was a part of who I am for many years too.

All those that had a huge impact on me and the choices I have made, Gillian as I have said, Ash Lawrence for running the MMS, that course was a game changer, as well as always taking an interest. Olly Chapman for help and support throughout that court case. Ash Tomlin for just sticking in through all of this. Colette for her ability to see through the fog! My MMS colleagues for all kinds of support and advice. Gareth, Leah and Lloyd for just being about, or working with me, and there are bound to be others I've missed. Obviously Sharon (not that one!) for publishing my monster.

And also the bands who make the music I listen to throughout all of my days, but whilst writing this book that would be mostly Big Country and Nightwish with a fair dose of Thin Lizzy and marillion thrown in for good measure.

And Gordon Corrigan for agreeing to write the foreword. An amazing client and source of inspiration and advice.

Kaye, whose imagination created the awesome artwork you see on all sides of the cover. Good job!

Colette Boland, Lloyd Smissen, Sue Mantell and Alison T Smith for taking the time to read this and sharpen me up!

Karen, for the lovely picture of a robin.

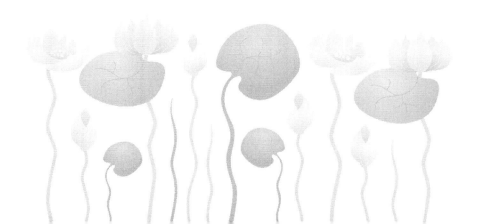

Introduction

So, what do you have here? What you are holding in your hand is the result of a three-year life changing hiatus. An unforeseen series of events that bring me to where I am now, not there yet, but possibly happier than I have ever been in my life.

My statement on how to be happy, simple really, take responsibility for everything you do, that's it in a nutshell, and have a little faith. I'm sure you'll work it out as you read this.

Who could possibly have known three years ago, what was exactly about to unfold. Having just returned from what was a fantastic holiday in Scotland, my son Ross and my then wife Wendy, I was on the top of the world and felt ready to tackle anything. Pretty good job really, as you'll discover.

There was a woman, a business associate, more on her later*, who loved reading the blogs I was writing, she had suggested that I should write a book based around these. I used to blog on three subjects, work, my observations on the natural world and music.

So, I started putting the blogs together, removing the musical sections and planed a book to be called 'a handyman naturalists yearbook'. As the business evolved into what it is now, it was becoming clear that this wasn't going to work.

In October 2015 I enrolled on a course to learn the basics of writing a book, both the writing side and the publishing side, by the time I got to it, the book idea was gone, but not the desire to write one. I left with a clear idea that I needed meditation in my life, but no inspiration for a book.

A lot of the people in my circle were writing books, so writing a book was becoming the norm, I didn't just want to write the story of the last three years; my book would have been just another book in a large sea of books. I wanted it to be just a little different.

Sharon, (Not to be mistaken for SHARON) who runs the 'get writing, get published' course had asked any of us in the facebook group, if we could read the first chapter of her book. I duly did and it was during these conversations that I put together the idea for writing my book. Originally I would write three books in one as it were, if I was careful, I could combine the three year story with how you design a garden and also how to construct a pond and investigate some of the life within it! I could see some similarities in all three sections, they are all a journey after all, the trick is in linking them all together.

As my thinking progressed these paths became two and formed the basis of my plans for world domination

After all, having a garden, or favourite place, right in your own back yard, rather than somewhere out in the world has to be the best place to aid you in your own healing in times of need. So here's my journey combined with my thoughts about how to get your head straight and create the best place to recharge, restore and if necessary, ultimately, as I said heal...

So if you like, the first part of each chapter is the transformational journey I have been on over the last three or so years and explains how I now run my business and manage myself and seek to keep my mind at peace and the second is how to construct the perfect place to be in to achieve that clarity, healing and regeneration. The design section is based on the scripts for the series of vlogs that have been aired in facebook:

www.facebook.com/simplelifeltduk/

and YouTube:

www.youtube.com/channel/UC65vbiBOlkoD9u_xoLu6sZA

They are still there if you'd like to go and find them. They are fairly brief, because you're bound to be more interested in the main plot I state arrogantly, ha ha! Ultimately, stick with it, or nip to the epilogue for a quick cheat!

I also definitely believe in divine timing, and it is obvious to me that the time was right to write the book and the components I needed to put it all together had aligned up at the right time, and the fact that you have this book in your hand means that not only do I think I've achieved that, but you have bought it.

The comment has been made that as I wrote my story my writing has improved too, that could be another journey! Wow, they are all over the place. Incidentally there are some words that are probably over used, but that I'm afraid is just the way I speak, and this is my book.

I hope you find it inspiring and informative, but most of all just a damn good read!

*just assume that every sentence has 'more about that later' and you'll be just about there!

Contents

Chapter one

Aug to Dec 2013
All quiet on the western front

Walking the West Highland Way was a life highlight. Ross and I had been looking forward and planning it for four years. The plan had its inception on a previous holiday to Scotland, we were staying in a cottage in Tyndrum, an old crofters' cottage, with walls two feet thick and only partially inhabited so it was all a bit damp, especially that week, It rained just about every day as I remember. Ross had remarked "why were all these people walking past the cottage?" When it was tipping it down most of the time.

Neither his mother Wendy or I had any idea at that time. Anyway, on the Friday, it was not only dry, but sunny too, so we eagerly bustled our way out of the cottage and went for a walk. It turned out our cottage was right on the aforementioned West Highland Way.

"Can we do the walk Dad?"

Ross was then nine, we had to build this nine-year-old up a bit, he needed to start walking some longer distances, and slowly start getting used to carrying a load. In a year or so we had started two days walking and included a nights camping. The first day on the first walk nearly killed me, I had the lions load and our kit was heavy, but we learned another lesson. We must buy kit, light weight kit. Any way we'd got to this stage, and it was fantastic to actually spend the whole weekend walking and camping with our whole world on our backs. I remember we had more food than we could eat, so we left it at the other end of the tent and at the end of the night it was all gone, lucky fox we suspected.

We then graduated to three days walking and two nights camping, this was quite a milestone because we figured that it was unlikely we would need to carry more than three days' food at any one time. It also meant we could walk a circle. We did a lot of walks in Kent, did quite a few both ways too. Partly because the view is different the other way, but also because many of the paths are so badly marked in Kent that we would go the other way to find the other end of paths that we had lost. We got so lost once, we ended up in the household tip in Canterbury, we got out, but we, well me, got a little worried, as you can imagine we've got a full kit, it's late and we still had to get to the camp site, as well as find our way out of the closed tip! Needless to say, when we did the walk the other way we were miles off the path. It was a shame, because the proper path was fascinating with great views and plants.

Anyway, we did our final shakedown in July of 2013, our kits were as light as we could make them, we had narrowed our packs down to the barest minimum, carrying absolutely just what we needed and nothing else. We were ready and couldn't wait for the holiday; two weeks walking and one-week family holiday.

Because Ross was thirteen the walk had to be planned very carefully, you don't venture out into the semi wild with a child, especially in Scotland where it could rain every day.

We caught the overnight sleeper from St. Pancras. That was a hairy start, there was only just enough time once the platform was announced, to get to the platform and find our carriage before the train left, but we had made it, we were on the train and the adventure was go.

So, Scotland. I've always felt Scotland was my spiritual homeland. I've always felt a sense of belonging and calm when I've been there. And it's always been the default location for holidays, I've been up many times. The natives have always been friendly too, I just love it. Not that I've ever been there in winter, although that's been more to do with when I've been able to actually take a holiday, than anything else.

It also has to be said the scenery is simply spectacular, you'll know this if you have seen Highlander, one of the greatest movies ever made, or Braveheart, filmed around Ben Nevis or Rob Roy which features the music of Capercaillie, a Scottish band that melds traditional Scottish folk music with a very modern sound. I just love mountains and valleys and lochs, I love the barrenness of many of the places you find off the beaten track. Have you ever driven and walked up to Loch Glass from Evanton, it's scenery to die for. There's an abandoned cottage up there that would be idyllic, I'd love to live there, but, it'll never happen for so many reasons, but it's still in my head as a possibility. Just to own it and spend time there when I could. But that would really annoy the locals.

And Rannoch Moor, the biggest uninhabited location in the UK!

And the fact that some of the peaks are forever snow bound as well as being higher than the clouds most of the time is just mindblowing.

It just gives you an idea of just how small and insignificant we are. Best take responsibility for ourselves then.

I love the stories and myths, kelpies and clootie wells and the Brahan Seer.

It's just a shame that we the English decided to wipe out a way of life that the highlanders (and lowlanders) lived because we didn't understand it, a bit like we did to the American Indians, but this is not the place for that discussion.

The whole walk was pretty much spot on, we've done three more long distance walks since and to be honest not one of them has come close to this one. We just got it right. The weather played ball for the most part too. We stayed on Inchailloch, an island on Loch Lomond for two nights and it was idyllic, we explored the island, played games and just generally spent seriously cool time together. All the distances were the right length for both of us and allowed us to have time for each other or even just read. Ross finished two books. Possibly more than he's done before or since. The scenery was just absolutely fantastic, we have always been in love with Scotland and to experience it like this was just unbelievable.

One of the most fantastic things about long distance walking is meeting up with other people who are walking. We met up with a fella called Ivan and another called Davy. Davy was camping with his son and had walked the way several times before and Ivan was on his second attempt having got totally rained off before. We had a few beers with them and many of Scotland's native midge population. Ross was on the soft stuff. We saw so many buzzards that we almost became blasé about them, not that you can ever really become blasé about buzzards, awesome birds.

Incidentally, just before and after we crossed Rannock Moor the heavens opened and midges invaded in their thousands. Or as Ross put it, 'one, two, three, sod it one thousand, two thousand, ***k it one million and...' We were glad we had midge nets (a kind of net or mesh coat and hood that midges cannot get through), the little blighters were everywhere, but the Germans we were camping with didn't have any and didn't seem bothered by them. They are hard the Germans, harder than us at any rate.

Another way the continentals differ from us is in their toiletry habits. At the end of the walk across Rannoch Moor there is a wild camp site. Wild means there are no facilities at all. We English like a little privacy when we have a call of nature, yep, definitely not a pastime for the public. Not so the Europeans. There was a river surrounding the site, and it was starting to rain. The first suitable site, and the second we abandoned due to piles of (human)poo. The third seemed suitable, we didn't check the vegetation surrounding the site too carefully, as you can imagine.

Due to the weather, everybody retreated to their tents pretty early, but we all emerged when the sound of a large engine came close by. It was a rescue helicopter, it landed behind the hotel we were all tempted to check into, but that of course was not in the spirit of the trip. All the crew got out and went into the hotel and then all came out about half an hour later. Could have been an emergency, but we all reckoned they had gone in for a quick pint.

The next morning was horrible, and I mean really horrible. It wasn't raining in the fullest sense of the word but the mist was so thick it might as well have been. The midges were so thick that in the time it took to boil the kettle they had turned the kettle black with their corpses. It was so grim we just broke camp and left, you couldn't even eat food without getting a mouth full of them. It was at this point we were so thankful of the Europeans dirty toiletry habits. If we had camped in either of the first two spots we liked the look of, we would have woken up wet! They were under water!

For the first half hour of walking we were OK, but then we had to tackle the Devils Staircase. A two hour walk upwards a zigging and a zagging all the way, it seemed to last for ever, we have our world on our backs, it's raining and we haven't eaten, still daren't undo the midge nets. It's tough and Ross is not happy.

Kinlochleven is the village we were headed for, it's like one of those places in a fantasy movie, you keep getting glimpses of, but it never gets any closer, forever teasing us. Eventually though, the sun came out, the midges backed off and we were able to set up a stove and eat.

The last day of the walk was also raining, most infuriating because we are pretty sure the views would've been spectacular. When we eventually got into Fort William, after an achingly long and boring road stretch, we met up with a couple of Germans we had been leapfrogging all day and they took our photo, before they broke the 'end of the walk' sign.

Incidentally the powers that be have moved the end of the walk to further through the centre of Fort William, we're 'old school' and figured the original ending was most apt. We were going to be staying in Fort William for a week after all and could do all our spending whenever we wanted. I was disappointed with the available merch for sale though, we were incredibly proud of our achievement and would have liked to buy something to shout about it. I did later buy a fleece and sew a West Highland Way badge on it, and a Ben Nevis one. Ross never did though in the end.

At this point it's worth noting that although obviously I/we did miss Wendy, when we had our reunion, we didn't hug or kiss as I remember, we just didn't really, or hold hands, or even say 'I love you' very often, possibly if ever. In my case this is partly because I am a Pollard and as I'll probably mention loads we just don't (or in my case didn't) show any great expression of emotion, very English. But also I think because after Wendy One left, yep, there were two of them, I had put some seriously impenetrable walls up. Occasionally anger got out, but often that was about it.?

Anyway, the walk was superb, a real achievement yielding father son memories that we will never forget, we also lost weight and I trimmed up. This Wendy observed when the three of us reunited in Fort William before enjoying a week in more conventional holiday mode.

One thing that has become a tradition is the reading of our journal at the end. We never share our writing during the walk and it can be very entertaining knowing the others thoughts and interpretations after the fact. Ross had a better writing style than me, but then he gets regular input, maybe he should write this for me?

The biggest highlight of the week at Fort William was climbing Ben Nevis. The weather had been changeable to say the least during our stay, but on the Thursday the clouds dispersed and the sun came out and off we went.

Ross and I went off at our now familiar pace, which was probably increased due to the fact that we had no packs to carry, but we had to wait frequently for his mother to catch up. She had not our recent history of walking and was finding the pace tough. It was quite steep too. Give her, her due though, about two thirds of the way up Ross decided he couldn't do it and was going to wait for me to come down. A shame, but his choice. Wendy, his mother was having none of it, she was getting to the top even if she walked all night and virtually dragged Ross up. He has her to thank for that.

The last push for the top was through cloud, the temperature dropped and it was a bit like you might imagine the scenery on the moon to be, albeit we could breathe. We took pictures and then began the descent. Wendy was failing by then and had to be coaxed to stay on her feet and keep moving, a night on the mountain side would not have been good. Again we only had a packed lunch and that was long gone, so we were all hungry, just keep going, that was all there was.

We got to the holiday cottage at 10 o'clock, which of course as anyone who knows me means it's beer o'clock. We had food and Wendy hit the sack pretty promptly. Ross and I followed not long afterwards. She stayed asleep for most of the next morning, probably due to exhaustion. Ross and I got up, went into town, found her an 'I climbed Ben Nevis' badge and had time to sew it on her fleece before she woke up. That's love.

On our return life still seemed superb, business was still on the up, I had always been pleased that each year had shown gentle growth, I was now employing two people full time and had a third on an occasional basis. The size of the projects we were taking on was increasing as our reputation spread and the skills of those I employed became more specialised and the next project was one one of our biggest.

I've always believed you should treat all people with respect and let them establish their own level, as it were. I still do, albeit with a little more caution than I used too. I met a woman networking, she was a powerful entity and a reputation for being difficult, however she always treated me with respect and although I knew she had fallen out with many people I had no evidence personally to find fault with her. We had done a lot of work for her and relations were good, she always paid promptly too. We'll call her SHARON which is almost an acronym for a phrase she became known by.

She was happy to recommend us too. In this case, to her neighbour Mr Chapel. He commissioned us to put in a new driveway. Fred who worked for me was a bricklayer, had already put in a driveway for us earlier in the year, so I took the job on. The project lasted 3 weeks and enabled my business to make some serious, well to me anyway, profit. As I said, life appeared to be good.

So good in fact that there was no reason that the success the business was having was going to stop anytime soon. We were making plans for an Italian holiday, the first time we had really seriously thought about going abroad. Don't get me wrong, half of the reason for that was just liking the UK. Everyone speaks the language, even if they don't want to, the currency is familiar as are the lifestyles. A bit insular you might say, but the UK has many of the landscapes and climates that can be found in many places around the globe. But well, Italy came up in conversation, and Lake Como was used for the home for Princess Nadala of the Naboo in Star Wars. Italy was also a favourite holiday destination for my mother. She would default there the same as we did to Scotland.

Also, for the first time in my life I had money in the bank and nothing I needed to 'waste' it on. It was nice to have that cushion, but inevitably the desire to have a new kitchen became foremost in our minds. We had had the kitchen extended and although the building work had been finished off we were still living in the 'old' kitchen which now didn't work.

So, on a work visit to the local plumbers merchants I had a look around the display kitchens they had set up and discovered that they had several available at a discounted price. And there was one I rather liked. That night I eagerly shared my discovery with Wendy and Ross. It was a few days before we could all go and have a look. Typically, they both liked a different kitchen to the one I liked. And as you might expect, the one they liked was more expensive. Ultimately though they were right, there was more of it and it was considerably lighter in colour too. Actually designing a kitchen with the available units was included in the price although it was more a case of making sure that the units would actually fit the way we wanted them too. The shop didn't need to have them out until the New Year and that suited us too.

Result, we were on top of the world.

The Design Bit

1. Questions to ask.

Hello and welcome to the simple life guide to designing your perfect garden. In this chapter we'll just pose many of the questions you will need to consider and answer them in later chapters. But all the examples will relate to my garden and the thinking I had when I constructed it, but the basic principles could apply to any garden.

So, the most important questions, what do you want from your garden? What do you intend to do there?

Do you just want to sit and enjoy a favourite place? Read, socialise, have a bar-be-que, potter, play ball games. Surely you want to attract wildlife? Hear water? What times of day do you intend to spend in the garden? Will you want any illumination in your garden? Is there a theme you would like to have in your garden

In my garden I wanted somewhere to sit and be at peace, as well as entertain friends or just entertain ourselves as family. Kicking a ball for example wasn't needed, but I wanted to include anything I could to attract wildlife, I find watching and listening to birds and insects very therapeutic, and also include some statues to give a sense of history and personalise the place.

And when you've answered these questions, there will be another set of questions.

The Design Bit (cont.)

How does the sun travel through your garden? How do you get to the various locations in your garden? What materials do you wish to use? What plants do you like? What plants will best attract birds, insects and other wildlife to your garden. Do you need to store tools?

Planning your garden can be tricky, but I'm here to help. In each chapter we'll take you through the solutions step by step. See you next time.

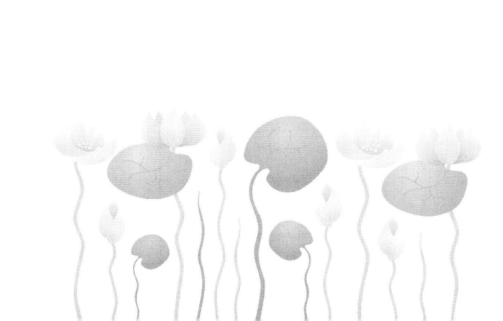

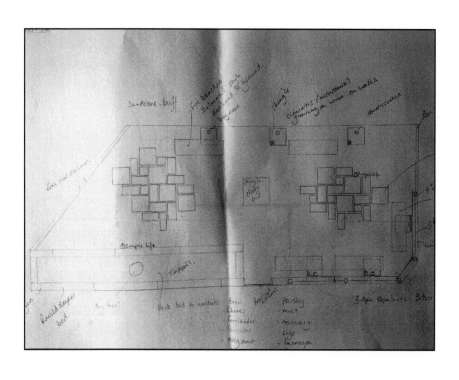

Chapter two

Rebound to January

So, lets take a step back, or more precisely a few months, back to January of that year. Ash had been working for me for about nine months and due to the power of networking and reputation, the business was growing so I was on the lookout for another casual labourer.

Wendy was working in a care home, one of her colleagues had a husband who was a builder. He was looking for work.

We had just taken on a very large driveway project that I naively thought we could confidently tackle. Then Fred came on board, which was awesome, he had qualifications and came in through people we trusted. We had already done the digging out, Darren had been helping us out on an infrequent basis. We called him the mole, he could dig so fast none of us could keep up with him, hence the nickname. If he wasn't there we looked lazy so we frequently had to ask him, to slow down. So the stage was set for Fred, as was the timing.

Whilst he and Ash were working on the driveway, I was erecting a wardrobe for the aforementioned SHARON and her partner. I had never made a wardrobe before but had constructed floor to ceiling bookshelves for some other wonderful clients, the Corrigans or the Majors, as we called them, they were both retired from the army, and this shelving had gone very well. This information I relayed to the client, I've never lied about my abilities, they trusted me and confidence was high, so I took the project on and off we went.

I remember sitting down in the bedroom with a pencil, paper, rubber and a ruler and thinking the whole project through, what the clients wanted and how it would work, how I would actually construct it, the materials I needed. I always enjoy this part of the process, possibly more than the actual construction. Nowadays I generally have others to do the hard work!

It took a fortnight and was great fun. Challenging in places, but that's part of life. During the build the clients went on holiday. On their return they excitedly told us how pleased they were with their new wardrobe, the year was starting to look really good.

The driveway was finished, and those clients were very happy too. They, like a large number of our clients at the time, were 'gay', it was very funny when working on the adjustments required to the gate next to the driveway one of them picked up a screw and passed it to me with the comment 'it's been a long time since I've given a bloke a screw.' Took a moment for the comment to pass through my slow brain!

In fact on one occasion I was in a clients house, there were eight of us in there, I was the sole member of the straight minority.

Now SHARON was the area leader for a business network, this was how we met. As a person she liked and got along with, she asked me to lead one of the groups she was responsible for. Group Leader, for the Dover meeting. This network had a script the leader had to read out which formed the agenda for the meeting. For people new to networking the script is vital, for those who are seasoned networkers it's, with all due respect, 'boring'. So between another group leader, Trevor, and I, we had an unofficial competition to get as far away from the script as possible. People had been sacked for taking far fewer liberties than Trevor and I were taking so we must have been doing something right.

It was whilst I was running Dover meeting that Gillian, who as you will realise was to play a large part in my life and this story as you will soon discover, first appeared on the scene. My marketing assistant, a fella named David had brought two colleagues to our group as visitors, Colette, a local marketing expert and Gillian who has a business providing hairdressing and massage. At the time she didn't strike me as anyone out of the ordinary, in fact I remember thinking, unusual nose and a fringe which to me she appeared to hide behind, a bit like Princess Diana used to.

Gillian has said since that I could often appear aloof or even a little unapproachable. She'll certainly tell you she didn't like me when she first met me. Even thought I was rude. Can you believe that?

One of the main parts of this network was the presentation 'slot' and Gillian was due to do one on massage, a Swedish head massage to be precise and I was to be the 'model'. Very good it was too. As I said this was turning out to be a good year.

Now SHARON had this 'ingenious' idea for a fund raiser. It would be based around a massage themed meeting, I and another group leader Janice were to attend the meeting wrapped in towels and people were supposed to pin money onto these towels as donations,

Gillian would perform a massage on us during the meeting. I was roped in; but somewhat uncomfortable with the idea, Janice said definitely 'no'. Gillian was worried that if anything went wrong it could harm her reputation, which obviously as a massage therapist needs to be impeccable. As you can see there was a little discomfort around the whole idea, but SHARON was, as I said, a powerful entity.

Again, fate stepped in, karma cannot be denied and once again SHARONs ability to make enemies quite quickly resulted in her getting the sack from her position of responsibility from the network, this resulted in the event getting cancelled and many sighs of relief were vented.

Gillian had joined on the reduced fee for a six months' membership package and when it came to an end she left the network. Luckily, before she had departed I had set up a deal with her to provide massage services for my staff. I figured that the work we did was hard and it was only fair and good for relations to put something back in, as it were. Obviously I included myself in this arrangement, after all my wife Wendy said I would thoroughly enjoy and benefit from it. I did and I can't imagine life without it now. It also meant that Gillian and I would keep in contact.

After our holiday as I said we began to work on the driveway I mentioned in the last chapter. Fred completed all the work, and was using his son as his assistant, this made sense as his son wanted to follow in his footsteps, they worked well together, so there was no reason not to. Although it was during this period that I began to be aware of Fred's poor timekeeping, especially getting to work on time.

Fred was putting in a path at another clients a week or two after the driveway. He didn't know that Ash and I were working next door, and he rolled in 30 minutes late. When asked why he just shrugged the question off. I asked him again later and he pretty much refused to talk to me. We often have reasons for these occurrences, but to understand I had to know why. If for no other reason that clients expect punctuality. The conversation became unpleasant and very one way, he accused me of treating him like a child; I was a teacher, but, well you work it out. I hoped that that was it and standards would be better adhered to.

The next day, he was due to take the works van to work. I knew time would be tight so had got everything ready for him. He was late again and all I said was, 'Am I not getting through to you?' He exploded into a long dialogue of foul language and left. This was all in front of his son. Maybe that was why he was previously unemployed. Apart from a few threats that was the last we heard of from him.

Enter Josh. Josh had e mailed asking if we had any work. We had a chat and he joined us a week later. Josh was a carpenter and boat builder, meaning his ability with wood was good enough that a boat wouldn't sink. He would be good for us, as he indeed proved to be.

It was during this time that SHARON called us in to sort some kitchen cupboards. On arrival, she and her partner had a brief discussion as to whether they should show us the wardrobe. Which obviously they did, they were always going to, that might even have been the real reason they asked us over. What they showed us had to be seen to be believed. Several of the upper doors had warped and the sliding doors refused to slide. I was quite staggered, but thankfully we now had Josh with all his knowledge in the field of carpentry We would send him over, although we were afraid that SHARON would eat him for breakfast, and lunch and tea.

The Design Bit

2. Planning your garden.

First assess what is already there. And what is to be kept.

In my garden, four trees were established and provided useful shade in the summer, as well as different colours through the summer and winter, a copper beech, a sycamore, an ash and a cherry. There was also a garden shed and an old pergola.

A new fence had been placed on the north side of the garden. There is an ivy covered fence to the south and west and an old brick and flint shed to the east.

The soil here is silty.

As I said in the last chapter the garden had two main purposes, firstly, somewhere to be, socialise and also meditate. There was also a mixture of sunny and shaded areas. One area, the pergola, already existed, and was sunlit in the evening, perfect for a bbq. Sun first appears in the morning by the beech. Both areas provided shade at different times of day. A section of decking was included by the beech to catch the sun in the morning

The second as I mentioned, a home for wildlife, more on that later.

Grass traditionally struggles here due to large amounts of footfall, as you can imagine, running a business and needing to access

The Design Bit (cont.)

garden machinery, the ground can get quite churned up, and also because the trees sucking up most of the available water. Ultimately it was decided to put in a path and extend the beds thus removing the lawn completely.

A plan was born, see you in the next chapter.

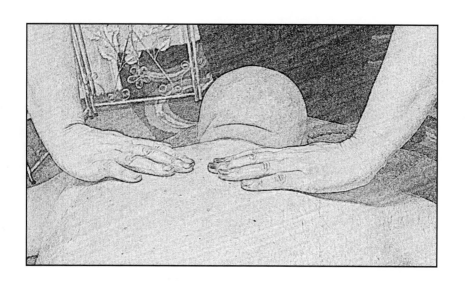

Chapter Three

Nov 13 to Jan 14
It's Never Just One Thing

Fred's departure was unfortunate, but really just one of those things that happens. I do remember Wendy coming out of the house after he had departed and saying, 'What was all the noise about?' 'I think Fred just quit', I replied.

Playing music has always been a big part of my life, creating and arranging music is a wonderful experience. I had been writing, arranging and performing with Laura, a singer, for several years. We wrote what I still believe are some great songs, but we never had any real success. It was in the October that she told me she didn't want to do this anymore, she was fed up with going out and singing her heart out for what was ultimately very little return. I totally got it. I still have not yet managed to find any long term musical solution, but it'll happen when the times right. One of the reasons is that I'm not a big fan of covers, and have got sacked from every covers band I've been in, I tend to have opinions...

Anyway, this call from SHARON (mentioned last chapter) was the start of the slide deep into the engulfing abyss that my life was about to become; do you like the dramatic tones?

Josh visited her house the next week, he got the sliding doors sliding better than I ever did, cool, whatever else I am, I've never had any problem with anybody being more skilled than I am. But two of the doors were so badly warped there was nothing he could do with them, they would have to be replaced.

Now, here's the snag, Josh had no money and he was working about twenty miles away from home so we had no trade accounts set up that far out at the time. And I was 40 miles away so I couldn't get there that day either. Now the whole world might have been totally different, if either of these situations had been, well, different, but they weren't. I made what seemed a sensible suggestion, ask SHARON for the money and I would square it up with her later via BACS, I still thought we were friends at that time.

Ten minutes later I got a call from our disgruntled client. She wanted all the doors replaced, and she wasn't going to lend any money....etc.etc.etc. so I arranged to go over the following week at a time to suit her, to discuss the situation.

Due to the character of the lady I took Josh with me. It was a very unpleasant afternoon, she now wanted a whole new wardrobe. We left and I promised to get back to her.

Bugger, basically, that's BUGGER, as in really not good. The doors I had no issue with, they were no good and needed to be replaced. But the carcase was sound, however the wood might have wanted to move or warp, it was firmly held in place by itself and the wall.

As a Libra I always think too much and often carry the weight of the world on my shoulders, this was the beginning of eighteen months or so that were going to become a constant battle with anxiety. I knew this would be the case, but I'm also a terrier and this wasn't a time to lay down and submit. There would be a battle to win here. As I would later discover this lady was using tradesman to make a living. And a friend Laura, mentioned earlier, who I had disagreed with about SHARON, now stated, 'well, like I warned you, now it's your turn'.

So creativity had gone for the moment and now we had work problem number one.

It was about this time Wendy and I went to see Simple Minds (awesome band from the eighties) at the O2. I like going to gigs as much as I like playing them and it was good to shed the anxiety that was building up. And what an awesome gig, so needed just then. I always said that next to my family, music was what got me up in the morning and keeps me going through the day. Love me, love my music.

And Christmas wasn't much better, SHARON had been rumbling away right through December, so stress was building and just before Christmas Eve I got a call from my mother. She had Pulmonary Fibrosis so was very inactive. She had a leak in the roof right above the toilet. Turns out it was a cracked tile. On Christmas Eve we went over and changed the tile, I could just reach it, just. On the ladder and at full stretch; but I got the job done. We went to get some fish and chips and as we were sitting eating them I could feel my back starting to seize up. By the time we got home and the evening progressed it got worse and worse, by the end of the evening I was in agony. Might have been hard work, but mostly I think it was stress. This potential court case was starting to really play on my mind. I'm one of the good guys and always try to do the best for my clients, I just had a lot to learn.

Stubbornness meant that I went out with Wendy and Ross on Christmas Day to walk the dog, but by God was I stiff. One good thing though, it meant I had a great reason to spend half my life in the bath.

I've always held a Christmas works bar b que which has always been quite fun, a bit of a novelty and so far, the weather has always been kind. This year was possibly the exception. My head was in a strange place, as you can imagine. Wendy was on a late shift so stayed just long enough to say hello. Josh and his wife came but it couldn't have been more obvious that they really didn't want to be there, even though they tried to hide it. Sorry Josh, but it was true! Del, a good mate, but not an actual member of the business had double booked himself and couldn't make it. He had always been a valuable asset to us, we called him the oracle, because he was a fantastic source of knowledge.

And Gillian came. As company masseuse, she had every right, as I remember she was hoping to be accompanied, but was alone. Ash was just his usual self and was off for a session afterwards.

It was a brief 'party' and to tell the truth I was glad to be shot of everybody. I was feeling glum. I collected together firewood for the fire... got some more beers and put on the DVD I had got for Christmas. Genesis Revisited. Steve Hackett had re-recorded and re worked many of the classic early Genesis songs and tracks. Just what I needed. I'd always been a huge fan of their earlier music, so it was great to just loose myself in the dvd for a couple of hours. The opening to 'watcher of the skies' is just so awesome.

Due to the horrendous state of my back, Ash gave me his massage appointment. It helped, combined with a long bath before and after.

I also had some of the most painful but ultimately successful sessions of physiotherapy, on the NHS no less. My doctor took one look at me and just wrote the referral.

It was during January that I received a text message from Mr Chapel telling me his driveway had a 'dip' in it. I went to see him and indeed his driveway did have a 'dip' in it, in fact he actually had two!

Del, 'the oracle' and I went to investigate, Initially, we thought we could lift those sections of driveway fill in a little more sand, compact it and relay them. Ultimately, as it turned out, we were going to have to lift the whole lot and start again. BUGGER!!!

So now it's no musical creativity, a wardrobe and a driveway. My personal harmony was on the slide.

I did little physical work during January whilst I healed, which was just as well. Ash was going on a plumbing course in February to enable him to improve his skills within the business and also carry out the plumbing on the kitchen we were about to install at home, after all it's best fitted than in pieces in the dining room.

It was whilst we were installing the kitchen that the court summons arrived. More stress, but once again that stubborn streak kicked in. Twenty-eight days to assess the situation and decide how to proceed.

So now it's no musical creativity, a wardrobe, a driveway and a court case. Slope getting steeper and longer.

I was still functioning, somehow and knew that I would also have to phone Amanda and see what her driveway was like, after all Fred had laid that driveway too.

When I made the call 'A bit wibbly wobbly', was her response.

That bloody abyss is getting bloody cavernous now.

So now it's no musical creativity, a wardrobe, 2 driveways and a court case. Free Fall!

I was starting to have sleepless nights, not completely sleepless that is. I would go to sleep fine and wake up at about two o' clock needing a wee and that was it, awake until ten minutes before the alarm went off. It didn't even matter how much I had drunk, or not drunk! A lack of sleep was adding to the difficulties I already had to deal with. The phone ringing was becoming a real fear, 'what else had we done wrong?' Phone calls were the life blood of the business and I just didn't want the phone to ring, that's how bad it had become. All added to that gut wrenching feeling of your stomach being tied up in knots, that this kind of anxiety induces.

But I would deal with all this. All these problems had my name on them. I had never run away from anything in my life and I wasn't about to start now.

But I was going to need help to sort all this out.

I had also stepped away from group leadership of the Dover networking group, leading the actual meetings was fun, but all the bits behind the scenes, was to put it mildly, tedious, especially trying to get people to do presentations. I took on the 'ops' role to keep my reduced fees situation. The operations assistant deals with all the admin and bookings etc.

As I said in chapter one, we bought a kitchen and would fit it in winter when things are often quiet. Should have taken that as a warning sign, certainly would now, never take your foot off the gas just push harder all the time.

We had our challenges fitting it and had to change several plans as we went, but it's just so cool seeing a project you've had in mind for so long actually coming to fruition. Little things like lights over the worktops, a real oak worktop, a ceramic hob, so easy to clean, cupboards where you want them. It was just so cool

Here also, was somewhere I could watch the birds at the feeders I had hanging all around the yard. Watching sparrows in particular is very entertaining, there's more politics in a flock of sparrows than in the run up to a general election. They fight and squabble all the time, and usually over the same feeding perch. Just like a favourite seat in a staffroom. But we also see greenfinches, chaffinches, great tits and blue tits on the feeders and dunnocks, robins and blackbirds clearing up what they can on the ground. Occasionally goldfinches too and you can never see enough goldfinches, they are so stunning.

I remember on one occasion Ross called me to his room and there was a sparrowhawk sitting on top of the hedge mantling a prey item. So cool and right in our own backyard. Privileged.

These are all distractions that help you keep faith in yourself when the world seems to take great pride in knocking you at every turn.

The Design Bit

3. Why Animals?

Here's where we get a little different, we think that encouraging as much wildlife into your garden is most important, and important on so many levels. Firstly, because so many of the birds and animals we take for granted are in danger of becoming locally extinct. Is that over dramatic? I don't think so. Sparrow flocks are up to 50% smaller, hedgehog numbers are lower than ever, many bumblebee species are dramatically low, and if they all went then it's curtains for all of us. Why is this? Because we are systematically destroying large amounts of wild habitats. Private gardens cover if not the largest single area of ground in the country, then a very large percentage of it, and where better to give all wildlife an oasis to exist. It's just connecting them all up for all creatures that's hard, they can't all fly!

OK depressing science bit over, whilst that's all true, there is another vitally important reason we should encourage wildlife into our garden. It's good for us, it's good for our soul, good for our wellbeing. They help us restore ourselves, and quite frankly we need as much restorative as possible. Many of us are finding life can be tough, if we can learn to put our minds at rest and have a fantastic place to do that in our own back yard, so to speak, wouldn't that be really cool. A chemical free anti depressant, think about it!

The Design Bit (cont.)

So! What do animals and birds need to live with us? Pretty much the same things we do. Food, drink, shelter and access. It's at this point in our planning we should think about our wild friends and how we can include them in our lives.

We'll discuss this more in the next chapter.

Chapter four

Feb to May 14
A battle begins

Now as I said, I was going to need help to sort all this out. First port of call regarding the drive ways was Fred, now where was his number?

Fred it appeared had vanished off the face of the earth, no answer on his phone, or at his door. No response to letters. His wife had also left the residential home where she worked with Wendy, so no easy point of contact.

To be fair I didn't shift heaven and earth to find him, they had already lost their house and were living with his wife's parents. The chances of him having any revenue to put right his errors were slim, and if he hadn't done the job properly in the first place, how likely was he to do it right this time. And the manner in which he left the business also meant he was unlikely to have any wish to help out at all. I think it likely that there were other issues he had to deal with anyway.

It was incredibly hard to find a builder who could and would help out, they are a strange breed. We knew we couldn't relay the driveways ourselves, but we could do a lot of the labouring, so it was trying to find someone we could work with.

Eventually we found Matt through a contact at the local rugby club where Ross played in the team. He came out and assessed the situation with Mr Chapel's driveway. It was one of those situations where I really didn't want to be right... but I was.

Matt was actually studying to become a surveyor, he'd decided he was fed up 'freezing his arse off' on building sites in winter and wanted a better cosier life. But he was still a bricky at weekends. His wage whilst learning was not as good as 'site' work.

Matt had many contacts, which was very helpful. A contact for digger hire and a fella with a low loader.

We started working on the driveway in May. Josh lifted and brushed of all the bricks and then Ash, Lee and I started digging out the driveway. Fred had not dug out enough soil when he did the work which was why the pavers had sunk. We had a digger, but I was just not expert enough to make any real progress with it. I quickly lost my bottle. Karl the low loader driver was very good with a digger and spent an hour with it. As with anyone who really knows what they are doing he was a pleasure to watch in action, and really shifted some earth. Good job really as he was taking it away.

Ash, Lee and I got into a rhythm and really started to manage to shift soil pretty quickly. Certainly far faster than I could with a digger, it was actually a pretty cool afternoon.

Funnily enough Lee had worked for us before and had recently got in touch to see if we had any work available. He had a new girlfriend and was going to be a Dad soon. His life had taken a dramatic turn for the better in the last few months.

He had been introduced to us by SHARON. He was then dating one of her daughters, the relationship was not an easy one and he often spent the night away from home, often with SHARON and her partner. The last we'd heard of him had been that he had just vanished. He was a little like a frightened mouse, chasing his shadow the whole time. The transformation to the Lee we had now was dramatic. He was obviously happy, you know, happy in a way that is just so obvious. He just had a real spring in his step and it was lovely to see. Had a very pretty girlfriend too and was going to be dad. Also having got away from part of his past may have had something to do with it too!

The last time I saw him he and his girlfriend had just moved into a house, he had just got a permanent full time job that he loved and had a fantastic future ahead of him. He deserved it...

What a digging team we had made, we kept making ourselves tougher and tougher challenges and damn it, we made all of them.

When we finished off Matt and his mate took over, and speaking to Mr Chapel afterwards watching them lay bricks was unbelievable, the way they went at it was apparently rapid.

The only downer for me was that when I wasn't there the supply of snacks from the Chapels was far better than when I was. I'm sure it wasn't meant to be that way, just sometimes seemed like it. Oh well...

But what was really amazing was that we managed to complete all the work on this drive way without going into debt, at all. GOT THAT, no debt AT ALL. I have no idea how but we did. That has to be thanks to all those people who helped out. So that's a big WOW.

Now of course whilst all that was going on there was the matter of a court case to sort out. And right at that time this was scary, as well as bloody unnecessary; evil cow. Yes, that is what I thought, for want of better words. Despite all the positive things that were around me, and the people too. Ash went through all of this with me and he's still with us which is just so cool. I still wasn't sleeping properly and there were times when anxiety kicked in and just functioning was hard.

I often woke around two a.m., and its funny I absolutely love and hate, that time of night. I have come up with some of my most amazing ideas and solutions then, but the payoff is that your mind can also make mountains out of mole hills which was often the case at this time. Whatever it was, was never as bad, in the morning.

You never really know all the skills of the people who are around you until you ask and start looking. Being a country boy and loving the country lifestyle and all that goes with it meant that I had enjoyed helping out on the local shooting estate as a beater on shoot days. I especially enjoyed the sloe gin and sausages at elevenses, but that's a whole other story.

I digress. The gentleman who ran the 'pickers up', i.e. those who run the dogs that 'pick up' the fallen birds, Ollie, was a retired council officer and had been responsible for the historic buildings that are in the councils care. I gave him a call, figuring he might know someone able to sort through all the stuff I had and make a suitable defence. On being asked his words were something like, 'oh good I love a good court case'. He instructed me not to worry and that we'd be able to sort it all out.

He came over and we went through all the court papers so as to 'flush out the devil, that was in the details', as he put it. Throughout many e mails I constructed a 'chronology,' a time line of all events which I submitted to the court. I think version four was the one we used.

One of the sections on the court papers was about mediation. It clearly stated that you should only only tick the box for mediation, if you were prepared to 'meet the other party in the middle'. I ticked the box!

Now, after SHARONS demise from the old network she had discovered the ABC network that was beginning to raise it's head in Kent. The old Network was a network open to all businesses and not just to one member from all business types, it had an annual fee plus the cost of breakfasts. To entice people in it had a special offer, two hundred days for two hundred quid, as I mentioned earlier. ABC was similar, but there was no annual fee and no script. It was probable that ABC spelt the end for the old network in Kent although it is still hanging on, just. ABC was the brainchild of a man called Ash Lawrence.

I went to the ABC Network when Ash launched the Thanet Group. It was OK but on a philosophy of if it ain't broke, don't fix it I stayed with the old network.

Also, during that summer I had joined a covers band, BLACK ICE. Traditionally I get sacked from covers bands, having always enjoyed writing and arranging songs, rather than just doing carbon copies. I always felt that if you were going to do a cover, do something with it! Ultimately this was the case here too, but they provided a useful diversion from events at the time, three of us often put the world to rights after practice nights.

Anyway, one of the songs the band played was 'chasing cars' by snow patrol. Laura and I had covered this so I had a bass line based on the main riff. I suggested we do a version based on this and it was welcomed open heartedly, WOW I thought. Freed from the main riff, the guitarist Adam came up with some amazing atmospheric ideas. I felt we had really raised the game for this song. It should be said that Adam can really play, he has a fantastic talent.

I was buoyed up by the possibilities, if you're going to do covers then, as I said, do something with them, be creative. The following week we played it again, the singer was having difficulties, we changed it many different ways and eventually once again we nailed it. We had a guest in the room that night, it is my opinion that her dislike of anything other than the original had a large effect on the singer, I don't know, but at the next gig, my first, she flatly refused to have anything to do with the song and I knew right then that my tenure with the band was likely to be short.

The Design Bit

4. Wildlife, getting specific.

Birds, easy to see, hear and enjoy. Food easy, seeds, nuts, fatballs and mealworms to name a few. Put out a selection and find out what your local birds like best. We mostly out out mixed bird seed, black sunflower seeds and fatballs. Put them where you can watch. There's more politics in a flock of sparrows than in the run up to a general election.

Bird baths, pleasing to the eye and vital for birds. Have you ever watched a birds splashing about? I don't know if they do 'happy', but they certainly look like they do! Bird baths come in a variety of shapes and sizes and themes too.

Bird boxes, should be put up in the autumn, face southeast and be clear of predators. Why south east? Well do you want a north or east wind blowing in the front door? No well nor do birds. Not south or west because any inhabitants in summer will bake, south east provides just the right amount of heat.

Terrestrial animals, hedgehogs will be starting to think about hibernation in the autumn and hedgehog houses, like bird boxes, are easily made or purchased. Alternatively, leave some wood cuttings and leaves in a corner, somewhere an animal can burrow into and find shelter. Also, make sure that a hedgehog can get into your garden, more on that later.

The Design Bit (cont.)

Invertebrates come in many shapes and sizes and can live in and out of water, and often both, if you want to see dragonflies for example, you will need to include a pond. Bees can be catered for simply with a bee 'hotel'.

And also the planting included in your garden will have a dramatic affect on the insects that visit you. Many are plant specific. Leave an area specifically for stinging nettles for example! This will give peacocks and red admirals somewhere to lay their eggs because their caterpillars feed on... yep, you guessed it.

And if you have enough space for a meadow...wow. Insect heaven , and so low maintenance.

In fact one of the best ways to make your garden wildlife friendly, just let it get a bit wild in itself. Let the grass grow a little longer, don't weed the beds to carefully...

Daunted yet? Don't be, I've just given you a chance to be a little lazier...

Chapter Five

Jun to Aug 14
The pendulum swings again

So, mediation! Court mediation is carried out over the phone. You sit by the phone at the appointed time and the mediator phones you, you have a chat about the relevant issues, he then calls off and phones the other party. The whole process should be over in about an hour.

We had three or four chats over approximately forty minutes, the next time the mediator called he asked me what I thought SHARON might be prepared to accept. 'Nothing less than everything", I replied

'OK', he responded and called off.

He called back within five minutes, 'I'm afraid you are right', he said. Now it could well be just my imagination, but he sounded very much as though he was thinking, 'why have I just had an hour of my life wasted?' I felt the same way.

Why tick the box if you have no intention of meeting in the middle, compromising? Not only do you waste the time you've spent on the phone, but also add another month or so to the time the whole court case and proceedings require. And this one was ultimately over a year from beginning to end. No end to the stress levels.

This for me was the trigger, the time to turn things around, stand up and be seen as it were. Gillian had, as I said, been on my case to go to ABC for a while. My monthly massages were good for my soul as well as my body. She seemed to have more of an understanding, or empathy for my situation than anyone else I knew, so she was great to sound off to, even if she was working.

Any way we were becoming good mates and discussing each other's problems. I remember thinking there must be a problem with one fella she went out on a date with who didn't ask her out a second time, had to be a nutter in disguise.

Right, back to the plot. Gillian said I really had to go to an ABC and she booked me into the next local meeting. Ash Lawrence himself was leading these at the time, not only had Gillian booked me in, but she had paved the way for me too. Ash knew pretty much the whole story and also, as a magistrate, offered his help in anyway he could. I'm not sure if it was sympathy for my case, or his intense dislike of SHARON that was his source of generosity, but whatever it was I was willing to take it.

I didn't see SHARON enter the room, I was too busy engaging in conversation as you do when networking, but her jaw must have dropped just slightly when she saw me.

When we were all called to sit down for the meeting to start, it was very noticeable that SHARON had one of the three tables all to herself, no-one would sit with her. My main concern was that I got to do my 'pitch' after her. A pitch is what you tell people about your business in sixty seconds. No worries on this score though, Ash left me right to the very end. I had taken one of our job sheets with me and as well as describing my business I also stated how we make sure our clientele were always happy with the quality of the work we had carried out. Topical I thought, and put one right across SHARON's brow. Take that, you see there was no hiding now, it was time to make a stand.

Gillian continued to stand behind me, offering an awesome testimonial about the work I had done in her salon and also spoke proudly of the work I had completed at her parents. I had no idea of the major part she would later play in my life; indeed, I am extremely good at missing that which is right in front of me. Gillian will tell you I am a details person and I am afraid she might be right. A cracking example would come from the other night; my son was singing. I focussed my thoughts on what the song he was singing was, not the fact that he was singing, which was really the unusual thing. And the more you think about it the examples are actually all over the place.

Rumour has it that after the meeting, SHARON phoned Ash and, well, I imagine, ranted at him, along the lines of, 'how could you possibly let him in here after all I've told you about him?' And that Ash replied, 'he's very welcome here, I know the whole story, and while we're at it we'd be really pleased if you stopped coming, as of now.' If it's true, I'd love to have been a fly in the wire when that phone conversation happened. I do though have a good imagination, chortle, chortle.

It was also around this time, whilst in conversation with Gillian, that she pointed out to me that this was actually a win win situation. If when we went to Court and I won, SHARON would never be seen again and if I lost, well two grand worse off, again, she would never be seen, again. I liked the first solution the best, but ultimately there wasn't a losing option. Again, starting to feel better.

It was at this point that the money plant I'd had ever since we lived at College Road had just about given its last breath of life. We did get a couple of cuttings, but that was all. I am not superstitious, but at the same time believe that all things happen for a reason, I had never been short of cash whilst the plant had been healthy. Funny how I was now staring at a financial abyss as well as the business shaped one that was trying to engulf me at the time, oh well. That was just something else to deal with, on it's own it would have been a big thing, now it was just something else to deal with.

That summer also saw us, Wendy and I that is, going to our second simple minds gig within a year. This one had to be one of the best gigs I've ever been to. It was at KEW Gardens and it was a picnic. Normally on the way into a gig you have to submit to a search, but as this was a picnic that was never going to be realistic. We traipsed our way in; if you had blankets you got to be in the section nearest the stage and the deck chair carrying brigade were behind us. The stage was close enough, but not so close that you couldn't see the whole show. Having a blanket meant you also had your own patch of ground so there was room to move about and dance too, which was likely, this was going to be simple minds after all. My main worry was that we would get the same set we had at the O2. Not so, we also got treated to dolphins, a song from the black and white album. A real favourite of mine! As well as hypnotise.

It was so cool to be there and enjoy Jim Kerr sitting on the edge of the stage chatting with the crowd as if they were on the other sofa in the living room. The mans a master of his craft. The other memory of the evening was one of the most comfortable mattresses in a hotel I've ever slept on.

As I've already said the power of music to heal the mind is immense, and as well as simple minds that night, who were awesome, the next morning led me to one of my now fav bands.

We got to Charing Cross and found we had forty-five minutes to kill. I bought a metal hammer magazine. You have to say metal hammer in a fake Scandinavian accent, no really you do, go on do it, it has to be done. Anyway, this edition of metal hammer had a free CD with it. Most of was growly metal, I don't dislike some of the growly stuff, but nothing on this album really stood out until this one track. I had to play it four or five times before I could let the CD play on.

It was a track called Dagmal by an Icelandic band called Solstafir. Often described I now know as the heavy Sigur Ros. Absolutely music to get lost in, if you get my drift.

And healing, well there was still plenty more to come.

On our weekend walks Ross and I had accidentally done a section of the North Downs Way NDW and decided we'd like to do some more. I planned a way to do the section from the west at Farnham to Charing. It was hard to be honest, unlike the West Highland Way, the NDW is not geared up for camping. But I'd found a way, the first night we'd sleep at my cousins in Guilford and the second in Merstham, but the campsite was a couple of miles outside the village.

Normally, we could manage four maps in a day and that's the distance on this second day. We'd managed to overtake a number of people up a very long and steep hill and felt good, but it was starting to become clear that this was going to be a long and gruelling day. It was starting to get dark and we hadn't reached the village. We phoned the campsite and even though I had a very exhausted teenager, they wouldn't come and pick us up, 'no-one is insured for that'. As we left the village Ross was so exhausted he was in tears, and I have to admit I was getting seriously worried, it was dark and I wasn't exactly sure how far we still had to go. We'd knocked on some doors, but got no answer. I was even starting to consider finding an out of the way space on the bank to kip on.

Eventually though we found the campsite and we had a fair walk to get to reception where once again they didn't really want to help us, it felt like we were disturbing them. The sign saying the camping and caravanning club, the friendly club; seemed like they were having a laugh. The bloke who was showing us to where we could pitch our tent pretty much just said, see that bend by the shower block? Somewhere over there..' Like 'thanks!" We pitched and cooked, neither easy when you're that tired, luckily we were seasoned hikers and could do most of it on auto pilot.

Ross' feet were ruined, I mean really ruined, swollen and blistered. And bless him, he wanted to continue. We figured we'd leave that decision until the following day. When I got into my sleeping bag, my legs were throbbing like I'd never known before.

The next morning, they were still aching, Ross was a little happier, but only a little. We ate and he tried a few steps. We weren't doing any more walking, so we phoned Wendy. She was on a late shift that day, but came to rescue her 'baby'.

Now we could see it, this campsite was just like any other campsite, mown grass, small hedges, trees, shower block, nothing special. And we didn't like the welcome we received. We ate, hung around and killed time until we knew that Wendy wouldn't be far away, then we broke camp, loaded up and boldly, well as boldly as you can with a limping teenager, walked out. We were supposed to sign out, but as we'd still been made to pay on arrival despite the situation we reacted as maturely as possible and just walked out. When we got to the road and knew we would be seen we just crashed. Ross was in much better spirits, but still suffering.

We did finish the walk, but we had to drastically change our method of attack, as it were.

What was most bizarre was being at home when you are supposed to be on holiday. Very odd. What do you do with yourself? Your heads in holiday mode, but you're at home and there are things you could and probably feel you should be doing. I don't remember exactly what we did, except for going canoeing on a sunny Sunday afternoon. That was superb. The world is a whole different place from the water. It slides passed in a kind of strange tranquillity, it's a bit like a slow train journey. You go through places you know but from an entirely different perspective. We spend so much of our time isolated from nature, but from the river you are as much a part of it as you can be. Somehow even more than hiking and I've done a fair bit of that. Kind of real life abstract. The noises of civilisation are more unwelcome, but somehow further away than ever. It becomes a real Wind in the Willows experience.

We then had our family holiday, camping by Bewel water. Amongst other things, we did complete another day of the NDW, and also had a first visit to Go Ape, as Ross feet had healed enough, but this was an unremarkable holiday otherwise.

On our return, the band had two gigs on the same day which was exhausting, one was outside at the Crown in Eythorne and the other that evening at the Railway in Walmer. They were possibly the two best gigs I ever played with the band. I knew the songs well by now and that always gives confidence. The second gig was hard work because my fingers were now behaving a bit like rubber. It was also odd because the whole of the rest of the band vanished, leaving me as Billy No Mates during the intermission. I realised why on Monday. I got sacked by E mail, cowardly bar stands. I have to say I wasn't overly upset. I have kept loosely in touch with Adam, the guitarist. I always felt it wasn't his decision, but I'll never know for sure. Ironically the drummer felt it was his band, he'd set it up and they sacked me because 'I was holding them back' and they wanted the band to go as far as possible. Shortly afterwards the band folded and reappeared afterwards with a new name and a new drummer, I have no idea what happened, but it did put a smile on my face!

So unemployed musician once again.

The Design Bit

5. Borders.

Once you have a plan; I like pencil and paper, I love the way that a design grows organically, but have reluctantly booked my self onto a CAD course because expectations are now that computer designs are best, but I'm not convinced yet; you will need to make accurate measurements of any area that requires materials to be purchased.

The amount of work there is to be done will determine the level of planning required, in this case a simple sketch was enough to provide most of the information needed.

Begin by concentrating on the perimeter, it makes the process simple and you can also avoid walking on anything you have completed or planted; whilst modern fencing is popular, we would encourage you to think constructively about a hedgerow, low in cost and simple to maintain. Pleasing to the eye and perfect shelter for birds and animals You can still include wire fencing for security, just leave gaps for hedgehogs to get through.

We like to include blackthorn, hawthorn, cherry, cotoneaster, hazel, pyracantha, and amalanchia as a starter. Loads of blossom and berries as well as shelter.

If you have fencing, you could consider a hedge for one section, or even just replace one (or two) gravel boards with wood that has

The Design Bit (cont.)

sections removed to allow animal passage. Although even concrete gravel boards can have a hedgehog sized section removed.

A good way of making a smaller garden with wooden fencing look larger is to paint the fencing black, when you have planting in front of it, it appears to move away from you. More about planting later.

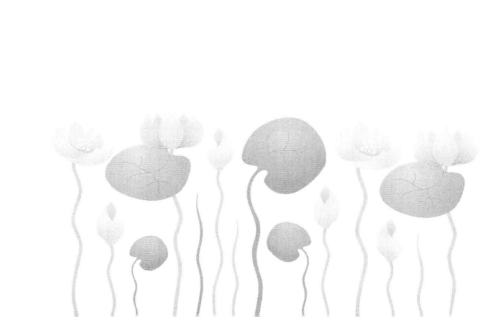

Chapter six

Sept to Dec 14
Court and cause.

And so came September and the first hearing. I was a trifle apprehensive, the only time I'd ever been in court before was as a member of the jury, which was rather different and exciting, no that would be wrong, interesting is a better way to describe it. But never as a defendant, and I wasn't sure whether there would be lots of people or what to expect.

Turned out that once again Ollie was right, it would have been just the judge, SHARON and me, the defendant. But SHARON, being SHARON pleaded she needed assistance due to her various declared special needs, claiming special needs was a favourite pastime of hers, so her partner was allowed in to help her.

Anyway, I am rushing on, the hearing was delayed, not the best news when you are in an unfamiliar situation, but you deal with it, I went and had a cuppa with a slice of apple pie. Funny the things you do remember. I also made a point of saying 'Hello", to SHARON and her partner, and Greg who was there. He was an aerial man, TV and broadband and the like. Turns out he was to be there next victim, sorry, willing tradesman. I did try to warn him, but.... Well that was up to him.

I am a biker, and so whatever the day was, it was another chance to ride my bike. Problem was I wasn't allowed to take most of my kit into the court house, I guess it could be used as a weapon. Luckily one of the guards was a very cool fella and stashed all I couldn't take in in the guards' office.

Exact memories of the first hearing are blurry in my mind, after all I'm getting on.... But as I remember, there were the expected questions and answers by both sides carefully marshalled by the Judge.

Eventually, the judge asked us to go and try to negotiate a settlement 'out of court'. We were shown to a side room in the court building. And there SHARON, her partner, and I, along with Greg had to try to work out an arrangement. It was almost entertaining, because however much it didn't suit her SHARON had to behave herself, indeed she was trying to demonstrate how upset she was, her partner was doing all the talking, whilst maintaining an air of haughtiness and indignation. Greg was cool, we knew each other and tried to be as matter of fact as possible.

Problem was, this time I wasn't interested in mediation anymore and I certainly wasn't going to have any terms dictated to me. A lot of manoeuvring was going on, and I said I wasn't having any of it anymore. I'd tried that and had the time wasted, besides all the efforts on behalf of the plaintiff were leading me to think holding out was a valid course of action. After all I hadn't miss sold my abilities or services, had responded to every request and answered every call. The moral high ground was mine, and as Gillian had said, I was in a win, win situation. Getting bullish now.

Ultimately the judge decided she would have to see the wardrobe for herself, so the case was adjourned, to be reconvened in SHARONS bedroom at a date to be arranged at a later time.

It wasn't long after that, that I had a fiftieth birthday to celebrate. In fact it was more like a birth fortnight celebration and it will remain as one of the last truly happy times of what effectively was my old life and the old me!

I don't remember whether my birthday was first rapidly followed by the MMS (millionaire mindset) taster day, or the other way round, but Gillian will tell you, attending that session produced a profound change in me. For the first time in nearly a year I could really see a way out of the chasm that my life had slide down into.

It had come out of the ABC networking events. As I said, they were run by Ash Lawrence and I asked him at one of the meetings at Canterbury about marketing. I have always felt it was the one area of the business I really struggled with. Sales were never a major issue, it was getting the calls in the first place. Typical for Ash, he responded 'come on my MMS taster day, you'll learn stuff that will help'.

Gillian was free on the appointed day so we both took off on what was our first outing together. As I said we had become mates and her support was unreal. She was just being Gillian, a helpful and supportive person to all she cares about, but it was just so cool to have someone who really understood the kind of pressure I had been dealing with all this time.

The two hours in that session were illuminating, I did learn 'stuff'. I had to be on the course. I couldn't afford it, but I also couldn't afford not to be. Several people I knew had been on it and as Gillian had said, (yep, there's a theme here), 'all those that had been on that course had changed the way they operated. I wanted in, and so enthusiastic was I that I signed up before Ash had announced that those who had been on that day got a cheaper rate. A rate which he still honoured.

Life was about to change.

Anyway, back to my birthday.

The first part of the celebrations was organised by my mother. She was deep into the throws of pulmonary fibrosis and was mostly wheelchair bound now. She wanted to take all the direct family out to dinner, so the eight of us, Mum, Wendy, Ross and I along with my sister and her family all met at the Five Bells in Eastry for Sunday lunch. We all knew we were on borrowed time with Mum so every event was to be treasured. God, it must be a symptom of how I've changed, my eyes are welling up as I write this, as the song says, 'boys don't cry'. I hadn't shed a tear for years, for anything. It was a cool time and the picture of the family as it was then, is still on the sideboard. It was the last of its type ever taken I think.

It should also be said that my mother was a 'force' of nature and would always do the best to control and organise all around her.

My actual birthday was on a Thursday, and as one would always do when self employed, you take the day off. My main memory of the actual day was going out for a walk with Wendy and the dogs. There is a foot path leading towards Hougham from Church Lane in Dover. I had often driven passed it, but never had the opportunity to explore it. Well today was the day. As is quite common, the weather for my birthday was stunning and this day was no exception. It was quite cool walking, well almost crawling through the bramble tunnels as we ascended to the top of the hill. You could see the other side of the valley, Elms Vale and the Grammar School and Astor along side. A town looks completely different from above, even from a hillside. You get more context for the locations. It's just so cool.

As it was October there was little in the way of birdsong, mostly just the occasional call of possession given by robins, with the even more occasional wren. It was the robin calling as the path levelled out and we found ourselves in a deserted series of sheds and out buildings, there was a lookout tower made of scaffold poles. Most strange, almost the base of a group of weekend warriors, or maybe a re-enactment group of some kind. I used to go and shoot arrows with the Shurland Bowmen and it was a bit like their woodland camp. As we walked further on the land became scrub, all gorse and brambles. Wendy and I climbed onto the roof of a long abandoned pill box and had a cuppa. Blitz our most recent rescue nutter, sorry, dog was most put out because he couldn't get up to us.

It was a lovely day, there was a breeze atop the hill and the sun was just right as it often is in spring and autumn. Eventually we had to climb down and just like the schoolboy I still am in many ways, I scuffed my knees in the descent. As with all grazes it really bloody hurt. We went back to the car and got home not long after Ross. I expect we had a curry and I washed it down with some beers.

The following weekend, the 10th Wendy was taking me away for the weekend, I had requested a visit to Stowe Landscape Gardens. We'd been there before a long time ago, It was during the Lawrence D'lagllio I smoked pot affair, a lot of nonsense that was, but it gives us a reference. So I was pretty sure we were going there, but I didn't know where we were going to be staying.

I had also been to Stowe when I was still at primary school and I remember being fascinated by the Gothic Temple. As I have got bigger, I won't say older, like all blokes, no ones ever accused me of having grown up, I have increasingly been fascinated with all things I consider 'gothic', from Victorian architecture to Pre Raphaelite art and the rock bands of the eighties and nineties such as The Mission, The Cure, The Fields of the Nephilim and The Cult amongst others, so this must have been why the temple stood out to me at an early age.

I just had a feeling we might stay there.

The whole of that weekend was special, right from the moment we left home. I'd bought a CD by Swedish metal band Katatonia, mainly on the strength of the artwork on 'Last Fair Day Gone Night' and as we left I popped it into the CD player in the car. We played it during all car journeys we made during our time away and it became a soundtrack in my memory of that weekend.

I had the directions to the rough area, but I was directing us to an unknown destination. At a certain stage of the journey I was given the second set of directions, and yes, LIKE YES, we were going to be staying at the Gothic Temple. This was gonna be just so cool.

The Gothic Temple stands in the grounds of Stowe school, a sprawling old private school, that is steeped in eons of tradition. It was also the home for many years of TH White, celebrated author of the 'The Sword in the Stone' and 'The Goshawk'. The grounds are full of follies and various themed architectures with grounds sculptured by Capability Brown.

But the temple itself, a triangular shaped building, with a tower at each corner, one that dominates the other two and can be accessed by a spiral stairway, all have spires atop them, a bit like a mini Oxford set of roofscapes. The views are just awesome. The outside is all arches within arches, gothic of course, and the intricacies of Victorian brickwork. And lots of windows. All roof edges have mini castellation's to them, it's just awesome. I over use the word, but well, you get the picture.

And inside, there's a painted ceiling, and a balcony. It's just so cool to look over a balcony into the room below, especially when your wife is there. When we opened the front door I took off like a kid at Christmas, this place was like a dream. A bathroom that Byron or Shelley might have had parties around whilst spilling wine and engaging in whatever with..... well you get the picture. I took off up the spiral stairs at a pace, it's so cool to be staying in somewhere that's so big you can run around in it and explore. Tear about the balcony giggling like a deranged dervish. There were two bedrooms, which to stay in, and balcony seats where you might read like the Bronte sisters planning stories of love and loss. And the tower top where I suspect the wind never stops blowing. What a place to defrock a maid!?!

And we were staying there for three nights. Made up? I'll tell you, and some...

Wendy had also been shopping specially, had some special menus planned and had also bought some beers especially for the weekend.

One beer she bought was the badger breweries Fursty Ferret. Whenever I have a glass now it reminds me of that weekend.

So, Katatonia and Fursty Ferret, memories are building!

We had the dogs (Blitz and Willow) with us, it hadn't been planned that way, but no one would look after them for us and they hadn't had the necessary jabs to stay at the kennels. I took them out for a walk as it was getting dark, it was almost surreal walking around this old school with all these old buildings at twilight, you don't do that very often, and I could also hear the sounds of music and voices from the dormitories, I presume, that the school children were staying in. Watching the sun go down is just sublime, I have had the great fortune to see it go down in some special places since and it is something I almost unconsciously find myself doing more and more, but I'm getting ahead of myself.

Incidentally the first job Wendy got was to clean up the floor, Willows first act on entering was to throw up all over the carpet. Got that, not in the car or outside in the grounds, but all over the carpet of the, I assume, very expensive temple we were staying in for the weekend. She always was very good at doing the wrong thing at the wrong time.

The next day we went to explore the grounds, not only did we have two dogs with us, but the harlequins (rugby football club) hoody I had ordered had arrived on the Friday before we left and I was wearing it proudly, all red, blue, grey, brown, black and yellow, so we were hardly inconspicuous. I should say the grounds are owned by the National Trust, well the ticket lady obviously knew we hadn't come in through the usual channels and we got confronted. Funny really, when she realised the situation we had a good laugh about it.

I've grown out of it now, but I have always bought programmes where ever I've been, at gigs as well as tourist attractions. I didn't by one at Stowe because I was sure I had one at home. On our return I searched, but no, I was mistaken, and funnily enough I still haven't bought one. Mind there was a very good TV programme about the place so I guess I didn't need to.

We walked every square inch of the place, took photos of every view and vista in an exhaustive search intent on not missing anything, tugged relentlessly by Blitz and Willow. I think I probably resembled an orang utan by the end of the day, still they wouldn't need another walk that evening.

The one thing missing from the temple was an open fire. I'm not sure where they would've put one mind, but I'm sure if someone put their mind to it it could be worked out, but a building of that character needs the smell of woodsmoke and the crackle of a fire to really send that 'gothic' thing off to a tee! And without a TV, a very healthy' omission, plenty of time is best spent reading, I read a large amount of Cassandra Clares 'City of ashes' the second part of 'the immortal instruments'. And did I mention I might have drunk the odd bottle of beer too.

One other seriously strong contender for symbol of the weekend is the red kite. Like the buzzard, another success story, red kites are expanding their territories, we even see them at home from time to time. Red kites are a spectacular raptor, or bird of prey as those less enthusiastic will call them. Often seen almost 'hovering' along the M40 they were just as visible at Stowe. Most noticeable for their forked tails, the only raptor in this country to have one, but also for their bright colours, their red browns, whites and greys. A most handsome bird and one of my favourites. In fact they were so common during our stay they also became a prominent reminder of the weekend.

So, Katatonia, Fursty Ferret (lots of) and red kites, quite a few too; definitely on the up!

In fact the red kite on my left arm was inked in the December of that year as a permanent reminder of an amazingly fantastic weekend. Great companion for the buzzard and Raven on my right arm from the West Highland Way and Ben Nevis.

I didn't manage to get into that bath until Monday morning, I had tried on the Sunday, but we'd managed to use up most of the hot water. At home we have a combi boiler, so are used to unlimited hot water on tap, so to speak. I didn't get long in there though, we had to be out by ten I think it was. You don't often get to soak in a bath in a room such as that, with the awesome ceiling in the main living room, you kind of feel this one should have been painted too, the opulence should have been throughout!

We had to leave quickly. Not that we had to leave quickly, but the time there had been just so superb. I mean really superb, one of the best weekends of my life, and I really didn't want to go. A bit like launching yourself into mid air, like you do at Go Ape, if you spend too much time thinking about it, it becomes much harder, so we had to just leave. I remember looking back as I shut the gate as we left. One final glance and then back into the car and off, no looking back.

One final treat, and one I have repeated many times, cream tea at Shelleys in Chilham, lovely old Tudor building in one of the most unspoilt villages anywhere. The village is on top of a hill which you can drive up, but it is, I believe, better to park just outside the village and walk in. Thus you get a real flavour of the place, I think every building has what we like to call character, all wooden frames and wattle and daub walls. I think they've filmed a "Miss Marple" there, you'd certainly expect to see her appear from round a corner.

It's also where Emma Ford spent her childhood and teens, you get a real flavour of the place, the castle and its grounds through her book, 'Fledgling days'. The book is laugh out loud funny sometimes, it also becomes a familiar friend the way the stories unfold as you read them.

Anyway, One of the two Shelleys tea rooms is in Chilham and the cream teas are just superb. It's just so English to sit in the village square eating a cream tea and these scones are to die for too, almost a meal in themselves. Any excuse to go there is found, always.

And then home and back to real life.

I really had managed to leave all the baggage I had been carrying all this time at home, the weekend had really let me have a break from the constant stomach churning I had been dealing with, which was just as well really, there was the second driveway to come!

Josh had left us during the summer, it turned out not one new employee would pass probation for the next two years. We had found a really promising replacement in Joe. He seemed to be able to turn his hand to almost anything, brickwork, carpentry, general landscaping, etc. You name it he seemed to be able to do it. Just what we needed. He had been a real success, he had built a couple of wardrobes for a client and built a brick wall for another, built a wooden arch and put paving around it for someone else. We were beginning to trust him and feel confident when he said he could carry out a particular task and relax in the knowledge that the outcome would be to the client's satisfaction.

And so we come to Amanda's driveway.

Joe had been in the army, he'd brought his references to his interview, very good indeed they were. One of his skills was as a digger driver. After my less than adequate performance on the Chapel driveway this was a real bonus. He started lifting the pavers on Amanda's driveway in the beginning of November. We hired a digger and left him to it. He had instructions as to how deep to dig out the existing type one and sand and then the soil beneath that.

Again he was asked clearly, can you do this? Is it within your abilities and skill set? 'Yes', he replied. Again we trusted him. The dug out spoil had been collected, we had saved much of the sharp sand as we had before. New type one had been delivered and spread through out the driveway.

When this had been completed, Matt, the bricklayer from before and I, went to assess the situation as Matt and his mate were due to go back and finish the job as they had done previously. Matt had concerns before we arrived, the maths didn't add up, there should have been much more type one laid than had been. Joe had assured us he had done everything exactly as instructed, except he hadn't.

A tape measure doesn't lie; he hadn't dug out much soil at all.

That's bad enough on its own, but let's think this through for a minute. We've dug up this drive for a second time, spent money digging materials up, having them taken away, new ones brought in, and laid, as well as paying for the labour to do it, AND I've also got to go and tell the clients that we're back to square one again. Matt and his mate will do all the work themselves so we can ensure the are no further problems, and that they will only be working at weekends. So, it will be several weeks before they have a useable driveway.

A massive positive was just how understanding Amanda and Sue were. Although not on a regular basis we still run into them from time to time due to sharing some of the same friends and relations are good. In part due to the fact they were kept constantly in the loop and always knew what was a foot, or under it we should say!

We put Matt on our account at Jewsons and basically left him to get on with, and get on with it he did, whilst I watched the costs escalate, not literally that is, I knew that was going to be painful, but right now getting this driveway sorted was more important than the cost, so...

We also extended Joe's probationary period as his three months had passed and as you can understand, after the driveway we couldn't pass him.

Whilst all this was going on I had begun the Millionaire Mindset (MMS) sessions. The sessions were to become life changing. The first was mainly about psychology, all about stepping out of your comfort zone. I'll give you a brief summary,

Most of us are unconsciously incompetent, happy with our lot and not looking for anything more than we've got, even if it's not much. Some of us decide this is not enough, so we try to do something a little different and become consciously incompetent, i.e. we know there has to be something better, but we don't know what it is! Without some luck or input of new ideas or learning or change in our finances we stumble and it is very easy to slide back into unconscious incompetence. Are you keeping up here?

Here is where something like the MMS is so valuable, it gives you the support to push into the next stage.

Having been running a business that was having huge difficulties, both systematically and financially, you can imagine how attractive unconscious incompetence could be. Many would quit and go and get a 'real' job. Well, not me...

As I said, I can be a bit of a terrier and I wasn't letting my teeth slip on this one, even though there could have been, 'walk away now, no one would blame you' moments. I was sliding more and more into debt, had a business that was threatening to fall apart around me and a court case pending. I wasn't going down and MMS was one of the most important and timely pointers that enabled me to stick to my belief in myself and most of the people around me.

Then you have consciously competent, you know all the things you have to do, but none of them are automatic, you have to think about them all the time, processes, marketing, etc. and lastly unconsciously competent, you do them all without thinking about it. Joy!

Gillian was still battling away in my corner. I couldn't see it at the time, but I believe most around us could, Gillian will tell you there was nothing significant going on she was just being herself. MMS continued too, just as well really because it was becoming abundantly clear I was about to have to make another really horrible decision and the work we were doing at MMS, was going to make it a lot simpler as was the support of all there.

When ultimately the buck stops with you, you have to make all the decisions. Mostly that's exciting, but not this time. It was becoming obvious that I was going to have to let Joe go. There were just too many instances to let things continue, and Christmas was coming. This is where you just have to separate business from pleasure, remove all sentimentality and emotion from the decision making process. We were starting to look at the characteristics of the personalities of the people we have working for us and asking ourselves what we need from our employees. We are very clear about this now, but back then it was not so obvious.

It was clear Joe had to go, but when, let him enjoy Christmas and then ruin his new year or just get it over with? Ultimately I went with the latter and on the Monday asked him to call in at the end of the day. Wendy knew what was afoot and was supportive, she made sure she was out of the way and stayed upstairs reading.

I tried to make the meeting as positive as possible but we both knew what the end of the meeting would be, it didn't last very long. I really did feel for Joe, I liked him and I also knew he had a family to support. But business is business and he was costing us money, so...

And when the deed was done, say it as you like, I did just move on.

Anyway, with Christmas was just around the corner, we still had a driveway to finish. Matt had taken some holiday and Ash and I were full on just to get to the end. We finished in the dark, illuminated by Amanda and Sues Christmas decorations, on Christmas Eve!

I was caught off guard by Amanda, I don't remember how, but I left with a £20.00 tip, 'to go and buy a beer'. I was a bit gob smacked considering the problems we'd had putting their driveway 'right' and the time we'd taken to do it.

But if it was praise, I would take it, it had been a bloody hard year and the next one wasn't going to be easy. There were another couple of major events to come, but hey, I'm getting in front of myself.

I still had an imminent court case and I was several thousand pound in debt, but, and it's a big one, we had put two driveways back to rights, we had answered all our critics and every question or query that been asked of us. Dealt honourably and honestly with everybody we had encountered and worked with on any level. In the many hours of need we had had a fair few supporters and hard as it had been on many occasions, kept a sense of proportion and a sense of humour. And the integrity of the business was intact, well as far I was concerned and as you may have worked out, I am my own worst critic and being a Libra spend far too much time thinking and deliberating over everything, so for me that was major!

Everything considered I felt good. Roll on the New Year and let's put a line under this one!

6. To pond or not to pond, as Shakespeare didn't quite say.

We recommend including a pond and the larger the better, just be wary with small children, a simple fence can be included in any design if necessary.

The increase in wildlife will be dramatic. There is probably a greater variety of life in a pond than anywhere else on the planet, creatures living 'alien' lifecycles, looking more 'alien' than the leads in most science fiction movies and more different and 'alien' than quite often you, or I can imagine... Endless forms most beautiful, wish I'd written that!

There are many who will advocate leaving the pond still, but I would always add a water fall or feature of some kind, great for maintaining the health of a pond as well as providing a relaxing sound into your garden, great for a spot for calming meditation. Just make sure the pump has a really good filter so it still would acts a filter and anything living doesn't gets sucked into the works.

Don't place it where it will be in direct sunlight for the whole day and consider where will electricity come from to run a pond pump. There are solar powered features out there and whilst they are far simpler to install and are getting better, mains supplies are still by far the best option.

You can buy preformed pond liners, but we recommend a good liner placed into a pre dug hole lined with sharp sand, make sure there is an area that is at least half a meter deep and one 'edge' has shallow and boggy margins to allow wildlife in and out easily. Frogs and toads can drown despite being very well adapted for life in (and out of) the water.

Site the pond pump out of the way and make sure a qualified electrician does all the cabling! Plan this carefully, you don't want to see the cables.

Two further pieces of advice, don't put fish in the pond, they'll eat all the invertebrates, and much as the flowers are stunning avoid lilies, they can take over the pond very quickly. They are not even indigenous!

Exciting....

Chapter 7

Jan to May 9th 2015
Think life is dramatic right now?

That New Year started fairly quietly, there was just Ash and I on the work front, and at that time not enough work to justify looking for anyone else. And anyway, much of my attention was focussed on the impending court case part two.

There were two other significant events that January, one, I packed in smoking. Actually, that's not quite right, I didn't actually pack it in, I decided that it just wasn't something I wanted in my life anymore.

And the second, Gillian was part of the You Review, a collaboration put together by Deborah Turner. The idea was that they gave you a totally focussed and professional image on all the places you might be found on the web. Gillian sorted hair and make up, not much hair to work with in my case, Debbie did clothing, and Liz did any biographies needed. There was also a photographer in attendance.

Realising I could use some professional help in this area of my business and knowing that as a recently set up collaboration the YOU review needed a test case, Gillian saw a win win situation, and I became a willing guinea pig. We had a great fun morning making me look very handsome, not easy, and putting myself in what seemed like some very uncomfortable positions to get the 'best' shots. The end results were really cool too.

Last time in court Josh hadn't been able to attend, but this time he was with us, his current employers had released him for the day and I had also promised to 'cover his time'.

We met Judge Burgess and the Clerk of the Court outside SHARONS bungalow and all entered together. We then entered her bedroom and viewed the aforesaid object of discussion, said wardrobe.

Now let's take a moment to just take this scene on board, we are in a bedroom, with a double bed and as I remember, the dehumidifier was still there, there were also large boxes full (I presume) of stuff, the windows were open, to let out the humidity presumably and the large wardrobe. There were also six people, as well as those mentioned there was Greg, SHARONS then current Handyman/carpenter. It was almost a scene from a TV comedy show.

The upper doors it has to be said were very warped, but we knew that. And the sliding doors were very stuck, but we knew that too. All the usual questioning and pointing out of various issues were highlighted as you'd expect, Greg had voiced all his concerns and had to leave fairly quickly due to other commitments. A little strange I thought, but there you go.

Anyway, SHARON, for whatever reason decided a bit of character assassination was required for Josh, it all became a bit unreal really. One line of attack she used was to question Josh's abilities as a carpenter by stating, 'he wasn't a real carpenter as he was only a 'boat builder'. Josh had always had a bit of a bee in his bonnet about this, and quite rightly so, because as he then explained. It is a lot simpler to become a carpenter than a boat builder, qualifications in boat building come after you become a qualified carpenter. If you get it wrong with a boat it will sink! The degree of skill level has to be much greater.

Not satisfied with this level of questioning she then came up with what can only be described as a gem, and you really had to be there to believe what you were hearing, no really you did, we are back to that comedy sketch again.

Josh was explaining to the judge that in his qualified opinion the reason the wood had warped was because the room was so damp, he stated that when he was carrying out his repairs there had been condensation almost running down the walls, as well as other conditions a skilled carpenter would understand.

SHARON responded to Josh's comments about the damp in the following way, 'the reason the room was damp was because Josh was fat and he sweated a lot'. Now did you get that, in front of a Judge, in what was still a court hearing, SHARON said to Josh, 'the reason the room was damp was because Josh was fat and he sweated a lot'. I couldn't believe what I was hearing and nor could Josh. The Judge was none to amused either.

Josh responded with 'Don't you think that's a bit rude?'

It was all a bit surreal, the Judge calmly played the situation down and moved discussion on and at the end of this process we adjourned to let us all travel back to the courtroom.

I remember talking with Josh as we travelled, it was all actually becoming rather fun, I was almost starting to enjoy it, dare I say. I always had Gillian's comments in the back of my mind, Win or lose the case I would still win because I was the person who had stood up to SHARON and said NO!

Anyway, back to the courtroom, the Judge decided to let us all in, Josh as well, normally he would have been called in and questioned and then left, but in context of the morning and his invaluable opinion, didn't make much sense.

There was nothing unusual in the courtroom to include, many questions were asked, debated and answered. I do remember SHARON becoming more and more concerned as proceedings progressed and I started to believe, rather than just hope, that I might just prevail, as I said I was kind of perversely starting to enjoy the whole process. I felt that as I had never misled SHARON about my abilities, and was utterly prepared to put right all that I felt was justly in need of replacement. I had done all that could be reasonably expected of me, so, ultimately when all discussion had effectively come to an end, and the Judge asked us if we had anything else to add and we all said 'no'.

The judge took a few minutes to deliberate and then give her verdict.

The short version is, we lost! It was funny, the Judge gave her verdict. She then promptly left through a door behind where she was sitting, SHARON, got up in tears and left through the courtroom entrance and Josh and I remained sitting there, slightly bemused.

'I think we lost that one!, I said, and rather more leisurely we also left. I dropped Josh home and probably had a beer, I don't remember now.

Now, I could be wrong, and obviously, the law is the law, but I firmly believe that if we had been tried by Jury, we would've won. If the

Judge had been able to follow her own instincts, we would have won. I think the judge was a really fair lady and if I ever had the misfortune to be in court again I would have no issue with her ever trying any case I was involved with. Utterly neutral and follows the law to the letter. After all the courts, don't necessarily give us justice, just the chance of it.

I had to send the payment to SHARON within 28 days or a month. I could see no reason to delay, after all the way I was going through money just lately it was losing all value for me. I immediately sent of a cheque with a 'with compliments' slip and wrote 'enjoy', on it just to push the point. Generous fella that I am.

Now it was about this point that I was really beginning to feel that life was going to go onto the up. The MMS course had begun with the fact that all businesses should have a set of processes that determine how they function in all situations, that is all employees whether management/admin or operations should have a written set of procedures setting out how they behave at all times; that is from how they answer the phone, behave on site and what they do on arrival for instance, to how I set an estimate or how we deal with complaints. We even have an induction policy now, it took two years to find a replacement for Josh who passed probation. You get the picture, basically underpin the whole thing.

This had several immediate effects, Ash's confidence soared, he always knows what to do, 'at all times', even if that's get on the phone and call me. He has become a highly-valued member of staff and can be trusted to make the right decisions, utterly. But we knew what to do if we found ourselves in uncharted waters of any kind. Each situation we encountered might mean a policy would have to be tweaked from time to time, and we now review all policies on an annual basis. Urgent reviews have virtually ground to a halt. In the last calendar year we have followed procedures and have not had one single incident we weren't fully able to deal with, he says proudly and with a little arrogance. And that includes those that you will read about further on. I had learned this valuable lesson the hard way. This business was never going through this kind of difficulty again. Business transformation made, well, mostly!

Another one of the points of the MMS course was that you should surround yourself with positive people, people that support you and encourage you, enabling you to move forward. This meant one of the most sour, negative, draining people was out of my life. It can be a bit of a balancing act sometimes because you can't always let them go when you want to, sometimes you have to let events take their course. You know that old chestnut comes to mind. You can't control everything that happens to you, but you can control how you deal with it. I'd dealt with this fairly well I reckoned, so now it was time to let all the hang-ups I had been forced to carry around with me go. Start sleeping properly and continue planning the rest of my life and the progression of my business.

One of the things that needed to be sorted out was the huge credit card bill that I had now that Amandas driveway was completed. Re enter Trevor the financial advisor we had used many times before. There were five months left to run on our current mortgages 'tied in period' so it wasn't worth the penalty for pulling out early. However, he found us a great deal with the Nationwide which would slot in when we got out of the current one. It meant we would have to extend the term, but the payments would stay similar. We just had to hold our nerve until July. Another positive. Definitely on the up.

Well maybe, there were still one or two entertainments in store for us.

One of our clients, we'll call him Colin, had some trees he needed knocking over. We had done several fairly large jobs for Colin, put in a base for a weather proof outbuilding, on a slope, so he could store his vintage motorcycles in a way that ensured their everlasting good condition. This one had taken a little thinking about, I had visions of the whole lot sliding down the slope that is his garden. We also capped all his fascias with rosewood UPVC.

His garden was large, mostly put to grass, large enough to warrant a sit on mower, which any fella will tell you is the greatest 'toy' going. I had a job once where I got to use one for an hour and a half on a fortnightly basis. So cool, going to work, having an absolute ball and then getting paid for it. Little things mean so much to us fellas. There is even something moronically satisfying about even having a mower that at least drives itself. Anyway, I have strayed from the point, his garden was large with many trees in it, well three of them had blown over, and he had a line of conifers that he was worried about after the strong winds we had been experiencing. We had to pass on the largest conifers, they were too big for us, but the rest were ours, no messin'.

I have two chain saw licenses and well a chain saw should never ever be thought of as a toy, but well, it's boys and their toys again. You show me the bloke who has a chain saw and will turn down the chance to use it. We have to risk assess very carefully, but if we can do it, 'bring it on'.

I figured it would take two days to complete the work, we booked it in and on the appointed days we rolled in. All went according to plan, until the afternoon of the first day, I went back to the van to get my workbag, and it wasn't there. It wasn't anywhere, at all. Not any part of the van, not where we were working, or in Colin's' garage. Ash and I, were baffled and wondered if Colin had hidden it as a wind up.

We knocked on the door and asked if he had seen it. We all searched with the same result. No bag. Colin had seen some 'dubious' types walking along the road, maybe they'd taken it. Figuring that if they had they would have taken anything of value and dumped the rest, the bag would be somewhere in or on the edge of the road. Again, we searched but found nothing. I phoned the old bill.

And they arrived the next day, we all sat down in Colins' kitchen and gave every detail we could think of, including the 'strange' looking walkers. No sign of the bag was ever found. The real inconvenience though, apart from the couple of hundred quid I had in my wallet was the time it took to stop all my cards and order new ones, get new reading glasses and sort out a new phone and SIM.

Now, I'll never know for sure, but I and Ash are still unconvinced that it wasn't a wind up by Colin that he couldn't finish off once I called the old bill. Lets just think about this, we are working in the last house in the village, i.e. we are out in the country, the van is parked round the back of the house and the bag is on the drivers' seat and there are no footpaths anywhere near. That makes for one hell of a lucky and brave opportunist. I know that wrapped up in chainsaw gear we wouldn't have heard much, but how many people would be walking past, would actually know the van was there, would go onto someone's property, and I mean right onto someone's property to a van that admittedly should've been locked, but wasn't, just on the off chance? We shall never know, unless he reads this book, maybe!

Needless to say, we now have a policy about locking vans, even when we're just around the corner! Goddamn it what's going on with the world.

So, with the Court case behind me, I got approached by Ash Lawrence at the end of the February MMS. The last leader of Canterbury ABC had given notice, would I like to run it? He was sure Gillian would be my number two. I said I'd think about it, and left, to think about it, obviously.

Well, all I actually did was phone Gillian and ask her and to my surprise, she just said, 'yes!' Funnily enough, Gillian had also been asked and had said she didn't want to run it, but would happily second me, spooky, or prophetic, who knows! This was the real starting point, and not just of our leadership of Canterbury ABC either.

It was about this time that we had to seriously start planning our trip to Port Zelande in Holland for the 2015 marillion Weekend. This is a convention that happens every couple of years and is basically just a massive 'love in' for all marillion aficionados. Port Zelande is a Centre Park site that marillion basically hire for the whole weekend and then book out the chalets to the fan club members. Three gigs, with no long train trips or car drives to get home and a whole weekend of marillion themed activities and events. We had been to two previously, but also missed a couple, so this was going to be cool. We thought we had missed out on the chance to book tickets, they can be in very short supply. So had booked the marillion 'not quite Christmas' gig in London; just after we booked that we received notification that the fan club had found us a chalet, did we want it? Just a lot! That would be four marillion gigs in four months, just so cool. There would be another one that summer, but hey, wait, once again I'm getting ahead of myself.

We were going with some friends of ours, Paul and Helen. They were going to drive and we would pay for the fuel, at least it was something like that, or pay for the ferry, not sure which, but we had to do some planning. Where is the best place for four marillion devotees to plan a trip to Holland, well the pub of course. And as is sometimes common, we went to the Berry, a crackin' real beer pub in Walmer. We had a really pleasant time, over a few ales and got everything sorted, or at least decided who was going to what, if it hadn't got done.

We left in time to get home and put the roast on. Priorities and all that. Somewhere in the process Wendy and I had the most enormous stinker of a row. I'm not entirely sure what happened, but I was in charge of cooking this one and was taking advantage in cooking downtime to do something on the computer and Wendy got involved, as I said I'm not sure now how the touch paper got lit, but I totally lost it. I'd like to blame Wendy, but really I don't know. I'd had a few beers by then and it was a couple of years ago. I am (I like to think), much calmer these days, but it has taken a lot of work. Anyway it would take me a long time to calm back down then. I don't think I managed it until the Monday. Anyway it wasn't pleasant, and Ross certainly kept his head down.

Maybe it was a result of having decided smoking wasn't for me, certainly smoking has a calming effect. In my case probably a result of the old dope smoking days, the body searches for these effects, I believe, long after the drugs are long gone. Certainly when I was smoking the first smoke of an evening was very much like having a joint in the old days, although the buzz would work off very quickly.

Any way the weekend was from the 20th -23rd March and the March MMS session was on the nineteenth. That is a day I shall remember for ever. I was so fired up for the MMS that the next news item took a while to sink in.

My sister called at 8.30ish that morning to let me know that she'd had a call from the Pilgrims Hospice, Mum had died during the night.

I'll say that again, MUM HAD DIED during the night!

I had conflict in my head, Mum had died, I was in a state of shock and disbelief and belief about this as I shall explain shortly, but I also desperately wanted to go to the MMS session. MMS had given me a lifeline back to a vaguely normal life, a way out of debt and all the problems that had found me, I refuse to say got myself into. Arrogantly I believe I am too decent a person for that, although there are some who may disagree. How could I honour mum and go to the MMS. The only solution; music.

I sat down and played Neverland by marillion. For me, one of the greatest pieces of music ever written. Lucie, our then Admin Assistant, came out having never heard the song before and was completely blown away by it. Eight minutes of transportation. After it I knew MMS would have to wait. I phoned Ash and told him I would have to miss the session. He was really cool and said to give him a bell when I was ready and he would go over everything at his place. I was also wondering, should we go to the marillion weekend, well only briefly, as I said to Paul when we spoke. Was there a better place to be at a time like this.

I don't dissolve into grief when someone passes, death should be a celebration of life. Also I'd had to deal with a lot of the emotional stuff at the time and I mean no disrespect to Mum, she'd have understood, this was just something else I had to deal with. Us Pollards do just 'bear up and deal with it.' My emotional unraveling was to come later on.

At this point I should back track a little, you may recall I said ' disbelief and belief', Mum had pulmonary fibrosis, basically meaning her lungs were filling up with liquid. This condition is terminal and she knew she was on borrowed time, we all did. We just hadn't expected the end to come quite so quickly.

My mother was a force of nature, a very powerful entity. She was a leader, not everyone wanted to be lead, but that was what she did, and she was bloody good at it too. She got a lot of things done in her life, especially in all the clubs and societies that she joined, the plant fair at Dover Cliffs for the National Trust is the one that springs to mind. She was gutted and relieved I think when she had to stand down as chairman due to ill health.

Ultimately when she was eventually diagnosed, and that took ages; there's me and my sister yelling lungs, while the NHS were testing just about everything else, meant that when she was eventually allowed home, she was permanently attached to an oxygen machine or cylinder. And obviously mobility was reduced. Mum spent a lot of time watching TV, although that wasn't a bad thing, she loved the snooker and we were a rugby family and she had SKY. It meant Ross and I got to watch all the England matches that we couldn't see at home and mum got to see her teenage grandson far more than she would've done otherwise.

It also meant, as all parents are, that I had a more than willing sounding board and mum had got much better at listening. If ever I was passing the end of the road I would pull into the village and go and have a cuppa and quite often just talk, 'at' mum. Worked out well for both of us. Nearly two years later and I still have to resist the urge to turn left as I go past the end of her road.

I remember one Friday morning that was very entertaining. The lady across the road was having a large conifer taken down, it was very big and had a telegraph pole deep in the centre and we were watching the tree surgeons take it down. Most engrossing...

Anyway, back to the plot. Mums life was becoming a frequent round of trips to the hospital. And she was getting sick of it. It was so common that my sister and I could have drawn a map of the ground floor of the hospital, I think she spent some time in just about every ward. Pulmonary fibrosis is rare, and women with it is even rarer, so she was favorite patient of interest for students and the like. She hated it.

When she discovered it was possible for her to be cared for in the Pilgrims Hospice she had her life's last mission, and when she wanted something she would move heaven and earth to get it.

Mum got transferred to the Pilgrims Hospice on the Tuesday and 36 hours later she died. I don't believe you can choose when to die, but I do believe you can choose when to stop fighting it. I saw it with my Gran, she died when she believed all those around her were happy, or at least in a good place. She had a stroke when Wendy and I were on honeymoon and died a couple of days after we got back. She'd held on for us.

Mum thought the same. She had also had to start paying for care and that really annoyed her, she wanted Sarah and I to get her money, not the carers. She also hated being cared for by other people, she'd always been fiercely independent in that sense.

So, final battle won, mum passed away. Again, I can feel the tears welling as I write this, but when Sarah and I went to the Hospice to see her, she looked more peaceful than I had seen her in months. No masks, tubes or cylinders or anything. It was just so cool to see her at peace and I knew that she would be glad to be at peace, finally. We had been so afraid she would die on her own, struggling for air at home, and she hadn't, that was such a relief. Me and my sister hugged, I don't think we'd done that since our father had died, so this was rather big for us.

There was a lot to do, but first there was a trip to Holland.

Paul and Helen picked the three of us up in the dark of Friday morning and we headed off to Dover to catch the ferry to Belgium. I love going to the back of the boat and watching the gulls and terns flying about looking for a snack, but on this occasion it was bloody freezing so I just made a few brief trips, as billy no mates funnily enough. The trip to Port Zelande is memorable for two reasons, the first, we got lost in Gent, but managed to find our way again using Pauls smart phone.. Wahay! Funnily enough we got lost there on the way home, in exactly the same place...

Arriving at Centre Park was the usual chaos, lots of people queuing and trying to sort out keys, blankets wifi and the like, and sort out the credit token system. Eventually we found our chalet, unpacked and just took in the vibe. I always try to take in this moment and savour it, the whole experience was in front of us, it wouldn't stay that way for long, so it needs noticing or it would get away.

Marillion, were going to play the whole of the 'anoraknophobia' album on the Friday and the 'marbles' album on the Saturday, and they were cool albums, seriously cool. I think I preferred the Friday night even though I much prefer the marbles album. And the production that the band had put together for marbles 'night' has to be seen to be believed, awesome visuals and projections. A real show, luckily the video has just come out!!

But Sunday was an unknown quantity, there was a bit of a feeling that they were going to play the whole of misplaced childhood, especially as they had t shirts with the album cover for sale. This wasn't the case, they played just about all the singles they had released, so we got a lot of the early stuff. Whilst I love the band just as much now as I did then, there are a lot of people who still hanker for the old 'fish' stuff. 'Fish' or Derek William Dick, had been the bands original singer, and had been in place when they had the massive hit single 'Kayleigh' back in 1985. Many people still don't know he left a few years later.

The three gigs were outstanding, but there are two other memorable features of the weekend. On the Sunday afternoon they did 'swap the band' where basically they play five songs and one member of the band is swapped for a member of the fan club. I'd sent some music in hoping to swap with Peter Trawavas the bass player, unfortunately I was unsuccessful. The weather was warm and sunny, so after a game of Bowls we went for a walk around the site at Wendy's request. Ross and I were chomping at the bit to get back into the marquee, after all you don't travel to another country to see a band only to not see them when they are on stage.

Secondly, Ross had become a convert, he had only come to go in the flume pool, which was seriously good fun it has to be said, but he totally got 'it', marillion that is, shows just how good a live band they are if after 40 years of making music they can pull in a teenager who's not into them or even prog to any degree. It's just so cool that they have some of the greatest commercial success they've ever had with their latest album FEAR.

And then back to reality, well after an extended stop in Zebrugge, the port building was large, largely empty and slightly surreal, but you kind of felt Doctor Who would appear at any moment. We combined the little money we had left and bought a chocolate bar.

So what was normality, Wendy was isolating herself more and more in our bedroom, only getting up in the morning if she had too. I wasn't overly alarmed although I did do my best to ensure we had some family time. You know watch a movie or all go and walk the dogs and the like. Well I am perfect!

As a counterpoint to this Gillian and I were having meetings planning how we would run ABC and generally solving the worlds problems. We were becoming real 'mates' and it was cool.

A short time later was the simple minds gig at the Winter Gardens in Margate. I had bought tickets, and then Wendy went and bought some as well. Oops. So telephone call to our 'ticket issue' sorters. Paul and Helen, neither were great fans but were persuaded to buy the tickets and come along. We promised they'd know most of the stuff.

I'd had a couple of beers and was really having a good time, jumping about and jigging about, what I do cannot be described as dancing. Nothing ordinary about that, except when Wendy went off to the loo a young lady draped herself all over me and stayed there for a few minutes, obviously attracted by my energy and enthusiasm, well, probably for an old fella. Don't believe me, just ask Paul or Helen. On her return Paul, or Helen told Wendy who was most unconcerned, we were pretty good together that night. So no one would've guessed what was coming a week or so later.

Incidentally the 'minds' were also superb, they recorded the tour and released a superb live CD, just like the old days.

That Wednesday Wendy had gone out to a friend of hers, I think it was her mates daughters birthday, she was late back and announced that she wanted to go out on the Thursday; I suggested that might not be for the best because she was working on the Friday and Saturday evenings, maybe we should have a movie night, or catch up with some stuff on the I player, and she agreed to stay home.

Wendy selected a gangster program, which I thought was a little odd, we never usually watched that kind of stuff, maybe because I didn't like it and she just went with my choice I don't know. I didn't really enjoy it; I don't think Ross did really either. I wasn't that great an evening.

On the Friday I was watching 'Salmon fishing in the Yemen', a film I had inherited from my mother. Gillian and I were becoming much closer by now and we had increasingly longer chats on the phone.

Tonight she was sending photos and stickers and the like in rapid fire over messenger. Ross must've been getting really fed up with it because he'd always been brought up that when you watch a film, you watch a film and put the phone, or anything else away, and here was I breaking all the rules.

The following morning when Wendy came home she announced that she wasn't happy and that she wanted to leave...

7. Hard landscaping.

A decision must be made as to what materials will be used.

Measuring all areas to be hard landscaped and add 10% for cuts, most paving won't fit exactly. In this example the area of block paving and the new section of decking was duly recorded. The decision of what to use was determined because an inexpensive supply of recycled pavers was available and the decking came from a garage clearance. More on recycling later!

Paving can be laid totally smoothly or can follow the existing contours as was decided in this case. The one consideration was that the path was horizontal widthwise.

Block paving can be very labour intensive, there are many other options available, paving slabs, shingle, slate or other broken aggregates, bark is also decorative and aromatic.

Beds can be raised using bricks or sleepers for example, breaking up the floor level can be pleasing aesthetically, or be to make actual gardening easier, one section of path here has a raised edge so that the bed doesn't invade the path, it cant be dug out due to the large amount of tree roots!

If a garden is on a slope then terracing can make the ground much easier to manage.

Next time we'll talk about planting and other themes.

Chapter eight.

9th May to Nov 2015
A period of calm...

Now you might've got the notion that maybe I wasn't entirely gutted with this news. Wendy had been isolating herself as I said, was becoming increasingly negative and quite often just put a downer on a lot of things, a lot of the time. It wouldn't be entirely fair to lay all the blame on Wendy's door, I'm sure she can tell some horror stories about me and probably has done. I imagine I can be quite domineering.

Wendy also had to contend with the fact that I was certainly partially a closed book emotionally, to put it briefly, when Wendy one, my first big love in my twenties, left, yep this Wendy was Wendy two, emotionally I put a big wall up and Wendy never really broke through it. Also on the MMS a large part of the content was all about surrounding yourself with the 'right' people as I said in the last chapter, positive people, people who encourage you and support you, and there was a part of me thinking how do I part from this negative person. Especially as I had got up in church and made some promises, and I wasn't about to dishonour them; and then I didn't have to.

I think we were both thinking it, but Wendy actually said it!

So yes, there was a part of me that went 'YES'. We went out with the dogs as a family, then went over to see Wendy's mum because it was her birthday. Then Ross and I came home and Wendy went to work, just like any normal day.

Ironically you might say, the last time I had tried to quit smoking I was finding it really hard, in the end Wendy went and got me some tobacco, told me to start smoking again, with the passing comment 'that if I ever gave up again she was going...' That's irony in it's most metally form, as Baldrick would say!

Ross and I went to my sisters for dinner that evening, we cycled back along Wellington parade and I remember being very merry on only three bottles of beer, funny really. I couldn't be late to bed because we were up at the crack of stupid again in an effort to sell some more of mums' stuff at the Barville Road boot fair, and Gillian would be there; because she had bought a puzzle from us the week before and alleged it had a piece missing, as if...

I had texted her the day before and told her I had some life changing news. She had been all agog, thinking maybe I had won the lottery, until we spoke on the phone. Neither of us had seen this coming, we may have quietly hoped, but we would have done nothing otherwise.

Walking around the boot fair that day was slightly surreal, neither of us sure exactly how we felt about what had happened, and unsure as to what we could admit to each other as to what might happen... we did a circuit of the boot fair, I went back to the stall and Gillian continued bargain hunting.

Later that day I messaged Gillian, did she want to go for a walk in the woods with me and my canine chaperones. I was delighted when she said 'yes!'

It was a dream like afternoon, I kept asking if we could walk further and the answer was always positive, the weather was gorgeous, we talked and talked, probably about nothing in particular, or the events of the day before, casually brushing against each other. Just revelling in each other's company. Thoughts about our possible futures, and disbelief that we could actually find ourselves in this position.

We were in Telegraph woods, one of my favourite places locally, I have enjoyed it in the snow, basking in the glory of snow covered silver birch and pine, walked it in April when the floor of the forest is covered with a white blanket of wood anemones. There is one section where virtually the whole wood just drops away and when you look back there's just a floor of white with the naked unleaved trees standing tall like rattly skeletons. A month later as the temperatures begins to become warmer being surrounded by bluebells. This is a wood that has to be experienced in May. It's hard to believe that nature can produce a blue so rich, but it does. I have photos of Ross in that wood at just about every stage of growth from days in the pushchair to toddling and later as a teen ager going beating through there. And then later in the heat of summer when the canopy of leaves provides shade from the scorching sun. And obviously kicking leaves around when they have fallen to the ground as autumn sets in, the greens having become that awesome selection of browns and greens and golds as the trees ready for winter.

It was similar to the feeling I had in Holland, everything was still to come, the biggest difference, this time, I wasn't exactly sure what.

Hopes and dreams and possibilities. A lovely dreamy afternoon that ultimately would have to end.

I messaged Gillian that evening to say that as I had organised a surprise that weekend, the next weekend was up to her. Ain't it amazing how different life can be just through a weekend.

Gillian gave me a couple of options and we went to the Duck Inn at Pett Bottom. There was an entertaining start to the day, I drove to Gillian's and when I arrived, armed with flowers, get that I bought flowers, personality change right there, I never buy flowers. So, I'm standing on the doorstep, holding these flowers, because Gillian's not in. I've got my best jacket on and have spruced myself up as best I know how. Gillian comes hurtling around the corner, ignores the flowers I've bought and thrust a bottle of engine oil into my unsuspecting mits. 'I need to put some oil in the car!' Said flowers got placed carefully on the ground, and whilst I top the engine up with oil, they get 'plonked' in a vase and off we took!

We began with a wander around Bridge, the day was just warm enough for a shirt and jacket. Again one of those where just being together was enough. Talk was easy and as we wandered we would brush past each other; just another heavenly day.

As it was lovely we sat in the garden at the pub after ordering our food. I forget what Gillian had, terrible really but I had pork, what I do remember though is that we were going to sample each others food, and guess what? 'Yep', I had some of Gillian's and then promptly ate all mine and didn't realise until it was too late. Shameful, oops.

The next few weeks were full of dates and meetings, we quickly became an item and soon went public which was cool. I remember one moment where I said to Gillian, 'I thinks I might be falling in love with you, is that OK?' And to my great relief, she said, 'yes.' Something else I hadn't said in a long time either.

Somewhere in the middle of all that I had had a meeting with Wendy, the basic result was that neither of us could see anything positive in pursuing a reconciliation, although I imagine there was a little surprise when I let her know that I was seeing Gillian. She replied that it wasn't a problem and that Gillian was a 'really nice' lady. Wendy knew her from filling in the vacant massage slot within the business. Well after all if we were going public, she needed to hear it from me before she heard it from anyone else.

It was not long after that, that we began divorce proceedings, which I have to admit is a rather humiliating affair. I appreciate why you have to go into all your financial depths, but personally I could see no benefit in deception, I just wanted it over with. The mediation process seemed to take ages and the mediator, a woman I knew and recommended we use turned out to be one of the most drawn out and patronising people I knew.

It was somewhere during this summer that I realised the money plant (crassula ovata) was coming back to life. This was a really good sign, I mean, to me a really good sign. I had been given it by a neighbour over twenty years ago and all the while it had good health I never had any money issues. As the business got deeper and deeper into debt, the plant began to die, it was a long lingering death. I tried repotting it, there wasn't much soil in the pot it had, I even tried watering it occasionally, but nothing worked. I know these plants seem to survive best on the neglect principle, but that obviously wasn't working either. Wendy had saved a couple of cuttings, and they, one in particular was beginning to make it, there were others, not doing quite so well, but this one, well what can I say. This was pretty major, a really positive sign!

Anyway, onwards, that summer was the first Ramblin' Man festival. I had booked three tickets after our return from Port Zelande because marillion were headlining the prog stage on the Sunday. When Wendy left she had been planning to still go, but she announced that she wouldn't be able to go, for obvious reasons I suspect. I had decided to take Paul and he was glad of a free afternoon out, I also didn't think Gillian was that keen, although when I eventually suggested that we buy a ticket, she couldn't get one quick enough. As usual, wrong thinking...

A friend of ours Gareth, who lives in Maidstone had offered us the use of his garage stating 'Mote Parks only ten minutes from here'. Liar! The day of the festival it was tipping down and forecast to do so for most of the day, so our planned jaunt out on the bikes was off and we went in the car. I had dug out three romper suits I'd had for fishing or riding the bike in the wet. Ross refused to wear his and spent most of the day wet and miserable. Teenager! Gillian found hers most fetching, and was sensibly wearing boots with heels, well that was OK Gareth said it was only a ten-minute walk. Sensible me was wearing walking boots and my waterproof.

All would have been cool, except we didn't realise how lousy Gareth's estimation of time and distance was. Approximately 40 minutes as I remember, and of course it was raining.

Still we still had a thoroughly great day, and marillion were really cool. As you can imagine Gillians feet were knackered by the end of the day with those heels. But we were victorious, if tired, we hadn't let the elements defeat us.

Later that summer Gillian fitted into another existing plan slot, the holiday. This was also important in other ways. Let me explain. As with the holiday in Scotland it was another two parter. Ross and I were going to walk the Hadrians Wall Path, something I had wanted to do ever since the holiday I'd had to Northumberland as a teenager and done my CSE project on Hadrians Wall. I wanted to do it then dressed as a roman, this time it was as a walker! And then Wendy had been going to join us, awesomely Gillian was happy to just slot in.

We took Blitz with us on this trip. On the train, and he winged for the whole five hours. He barely let up at any point. Most fellow passengers were utterly cool about him, folk generally adore him on sight, he does look exceptionally handsome. But it was a bit wearing. It has to be said he is very much a country dog and revels in activity. At no other time during the walk was he ever a problem. I was proud of him, put him in his natural environment and he's awesome, it's just anywhere else, still, this books not about him!

On the Monday, after a long walk up a very steep hill, well maybe not that steep, but we had been walking all day and had our whole world on our backs when the phone rang. It was Gillian. She was staying at ours to look after Willow who we couldn't take with us she was getting on and was very slow. Gillian had an ulcer in her eyes and needed to get to William Harvey Hospital in Ashford for an emergency appointment with the eye doctor and couldn't find anyone to take her. Not only was that a problem with getting to work, and as a hairdresser, working, it meant she may not be able to drive up that Saturday. She was more than a little distraught. She also had to put drops in her eyes at regular intervals, hourly for a couple of days then two hourly etc, so sleep was going to be in short supply, but she had to be on it or there was a possibility she could go blind, and for all the wrong reasons.

So, Ross phoned my sister, which was fun in itself. Think about it, Gillian in Mongeham near Deal phones me just outside Newcastle, I pass messages to Ross who talks to my sister who is in Kingsdown, near Deal. Anyway, Sarah's crew really stepped up to the mark, they not only got Gillian to Ashford for the hospital, the doctor and the aforementioned eye drops but also walked Willow for most of the week and made sure Gillian had what she needed to function that week too. That meant the world to me and when I thanked Sarah she just said, 'Family'. Which was cool, great seal of approval. Made up.

Life on Hadrians Wall must have bleak in winter, the views of the hills are superb, but in winter the winds would come whistling through, probably continually, they could be pretty fierce even in summer. I love going round a corner on seeing a whole new view, a change in the ruggedness, or a lake, or a forest upon the hill top. And there is so much wall still there. Especially in the middle section. It might not all be genuine, but it is still evocative of what the original might've been like, if you shut your eyes you can just about hear the roman army and the shouts of men and the neighing of horses. I love it. There are many stories of that walk but again, this is not the place for them, suffice to say that when Gillian arrived in Bowness on Solway it was just so superb for so many reasons.

Now this was a great holiday and a change of routine, location and usual thinking etc. is always a great thing, but this had a couple of extras other than the first time Gillian and I (and Ross) had actually spent a long time in each others space. One of the things that is involved when you begin a relationship with people of a certain age is that you tend to carry 'buttons' that have been instilled by those people in our past. One evening Gillian was sitting in the place I had started to feel I rather liked. I asked Gillian if she'd move along, or budge up, innocuously, I thought, she got up most explosively and instead of just shuffling up went and sat on another seat entirely, then proceeded to send me to Coventry for the entire evening. I was also trying to sleep on the other side of the bed each because she had difficulty sleeping on what she considered the 'wrong' side. That night she went to sleep on that said wrong side. This one wasn't me, there are other times when I did cause the problem, but this was me ticking a box that had triggered a response from her past!

This is best put into context by the helmet incident. When Ross and I had been walking the walk we had popped into Birdoswald Roman Fort to look for a cap. I'd left mine at home and when you are a, used to one and b, used to it keeping the sun out of the eyes, you really miss it. We couldn't find one anywhere, but at Birdoswald they had a Centurions helmet. I wanted one, it was really cool. I ummed and ahhed about it for a few days. In the past I would have had the micky taken out of me rotten for wanting to buy it and put it on display at home. Indeed, when I announced my intentions Ross did; but Gillian didn't, straight away she started thinking about where we might put it and then how we could decorate wherever it ended up at home. This was so cool; this was one of the contributions to the conclusion that this woman was for keeping. Then, as now, the support I get from Gillian is immense, and so immense because it's active support, not just passive. That is just so cool.

It was somewhere during that summer that I further honed the direction for the business. Up to now it had been 'simple life', 'making your home and garden your favourite place'. It was one of those light bulb moments, 'simple life', 'wildlife friendly garden design and consultancy'. Bing, that was it! Combine my love of nature and experience gained whilst working for the RSPB, with all the teaching I had done in various capacities and the work the business had largely been doing since its inception. And there was clear direction and a clear structure for the business to operate within. An education section, I would give presentations to anyone I could persuade to listen, and since then, I've worked with just about everyone from the Brownies to the W.I. The design and landscaping section, and thirdly, the garden maintenance section.

As you can tell, I had begun many journeys just lately; the fight back against SHARON after the mediation, the real fight back in business when I began the MMS, opening up emotionally when I began my relationship with Gillian. There was one more journey that I needed to begin, I didn't know it at the time, but my fifty first birthday was the trigger that set that into motion.

During the MMS, as with any course there are books that are required reading. I love reading but rarely get enough time to read the quantity that I would like. Any way one of those books was called 'Ask and it is Given' by Ester and Gerry Hicks. Now, I was usually a month behind in my reading and at the last session one of my peers had announced that he had read the first fifty pages and he wasn't reading any more of this 'namby pamby hippy tree huggery crap', I was immediately very interested. It was the weekend of my birthday that I began to read it.

My birthday was on the Friday and it had been superb. It's funny, you kind of get used to receiving a certain kind of present, I love CD's and DVD's, especially as my taste is generally not mainstream. And my mother had brought up me and my sister to write lists for birthdays and Christmas, not that she ever looked at them, or as I was to discover, did Gillian.

I love Gillians random presents now, but then it was a bit of a shock. Clothes and aftershave, what was that all about? Anyway, we then went to Canterbury for a fantastic breakfast. Then on to Slaters, so I could buy myself a suit, hadn't needed on one for fifty years, but I was going to need one now. Well life was changing wasn't it, and I had bought a smart jacket for myself, totally unprovoked, earlier that year!!!

We went to Hythe Imperial for a spa session and afternoon tea, definitely not the way I'd lived my life up to now. The cleanest I'd been since Banja when I was in Russia, but that's a whole other story. I remember dozing outside in the sun... in October, and with Gillian, life was just so cool.

That evening we went to the beer festival at Crabble Corn Mill with Karen and Chris, some friends of ours, and my stomach started trying to explode. I was really uncomfortable, and it was just getting worse and worse. Eventually I asked Gillian to take me home, I was so uncomfortable, my head was beginning to ache too.

We got home and I climbed into bed, when Gillian announced that she was going to let me rest and go home, I was so gutted I couldn't say anything and off she went. I was so unsettled that I was now not only very uncomfortable physically, but really unhappy too. At the time it felt like one of the most horrible times of my life. I guess having started to open up emotionally I wasn't prepared for this.

Gillian phoned in the morning unprepared for the outburst that was coming, had the roles been reversed this was what she would have wanted me to do and I would probably have found that just as hard, currently we are nearly two years in and we are still working on how we should be best for each other, anyway... Off I went, and she recoiled. She came round later that afternoon and we eased the situation... a bit, she was off that night and my sisters' family were coming round. Gillian was also away for the day on the Sunday, so I was emotionally bolloxed all weekend and it took me a while to sort myself out.

So, you might remember I mentioned the MMS and a book, 'Ask and it is Given'. Well I started reading it that weekend. Just reading it was healing, I didn't know why, but when I read it all my concerns faded away, I concentrated on the now and functioned OK. When I stopped reading it, they came back, although not quite as badly as before. I also used the English Heritage card we bought in Northumberland to visit the Roman Fort at Reculver. This was pretty cool, but I would've liked it to have kept me entertained a little longer. The book and its contents certainly took the edge of an emotional weekend, I am a libra and I overthink everything. Great when it comes to problem solving of a practical nature, rubbish when it comes to trying to be rational with emotions.

Ask and it is Given was the first step on a journey that was to result in me living my life according to the Law of Attraction, more on that later. Ash (Lawrence) had said that this, ultimately, was exactly what the MMS was about, but he couldn't market it as that because all these 'hard nosed' hopeful business types would never buy into that. Well more fool them.

In the summer we had been asked by a client to build a wall around his front garden along with some cast iron railings and a gate. We used the same contractors we had used for the driveway. It had all gone very well, so we were really pleased when the three neighbours in the same stretch of housing asked us to wall up their front gardens as well.

I measured up the areas involved and multiplied the original costings appropriately and submitted estimates. All three were accepted and we booked the subcontractors accordingly.

When they arrived they announced they wanted far more money than agreed. I refused to pay. One of my MMS colleagues Lloyd was a builder and I asked him to come and assess the situation. Without any priming from me he gave the same verdict that I had reached. It was a shame he couldn't spare any of his lads to help out though.

So, I had to find some replacement sub contractors and fast, this was going to be tough, I became best friends with the phone, but the story was always the same, anyone any good was booked up until forever. I don't remember how now, but I found a fella who was available, checked the references he gave me, check the pictures of his work he supplied and even went to look at some work he claimed to have done, sent pictures to Lloyd and all looked good so I gave him the contract.

The Three Year Pond

One of the reasons we have good relations with all our clients is because we keep them in the loop all the time, as our processes dictate we must. Whilst they might not be entirely happy with the situation, they always know what is happening, the difficulties we might be experiencing and why. This also means that they will keep me in the loop too.

So, when I got a call from one of them saying they weren't happy with the new builder I had to drop everything and go look. Sure enough, all was not good, the pointing was erratic and levels were off all over the place. The brickwork I had been shown had not been done by the builder we had hired! He didn't argue when I fired him, he didn't even come and collect the tools he'd left on site.

The skills I had learnt in all the dealings over the last year or so were paying off, but there couldn't be any messing about now. The next contractor had to be good. My God I can find 'em.

So, back on the phones, I spoke to a very successful local builder I had used in the past, he had a quiet spot and could help out. We met on site, he gave me a verbal estimate, I had used him in the past, had explained the situation and gave him the go ahead to complete the work. I knew that no matter what, the work would be done well.

And done well the work was. Very well, but once again a learning point raised it's head. We now ask all sub contractors to put the price in writing, as a result of this job. Because I knew this contractor for many years I had always trusted him implicitly so I was rather gobsmacked when he called me and said it was going to cost more than he had said. Eventually twice as much as he said, and pretty much the same as the initial builders. I felt utterly ripped off, but this time it was by someone I knew well and had trusted for many years, I knew he wouldn't be cheap, but hadn't expected this price hike. He doesn't even need the money, he's doing very well, he knew the situation and he played it.

Anyway, we don't dwell on these things any more, no blame, learn from it and move on. We now have a policy for working with sub contractors and have not encountered this at any time since.

So, moving swiftly onwards. The book course. Get writing, Get Published. Run by Sharon Lynn and Lorenzo Guescini It aims to teach you what you need to know on the publishing side and the actual writing side. It was two days of seriously intensive information giving and it was intense. Very full on. Still here I am writing.

Albeit, not the book that I had in mind when I booked the course. A lot had changed between then and the course and even now. The main one being that the original idea I had, I think I mentioned earlier, 'a handymans yearbook' wouldn't work. The business is no longer a handyman business, we have specialised and although our work is still to a certain extent seasonal, it didn't work any more, not for me at least. I left the course not knowing what I was going to write.

But I did know that I had to meditate. Sharon had guided several short meditation sessions as part of the course. I bought the book, some focus cards and a CD of music for meditation. I began by letting the book 'fall' open at whatever page and then spent 10 – 15 minutes trying to focus on whatever the random topic was. There was definitely something going on here. I would let the book fall open with my eyes closed, and I would flick through the pages so it wouldn't favour the last page I opened the book up to. The amount of times the page with the very subject I needed help to think about opened up was beyond coincidence. Or it turned out was going to be relevant to that day, even though often I couldn't have known it.

And meditating was becoming an important part of my daily routine, soon 15 minutes wasn't enough.

On November the fifth, we had the second annual ABC awards. It was also supposed to be the Christmas bash too. Much too early I thought and thankfully that was only alluded too. This was one of the reasons that Gillian had insisted I buy a suit, it was a black tie do. The nature of the event meant that we stayed overnight, well we were going to drink a bit weren't we...

On arrival we booked in, and get this were asked if we wanted to upgrade to the bridal suite at no extra cost. OK, this day and age it's hard not to smell a rat, but we said, 'Yes', and off we went. It was rather nice I have to say. Four poster bed, crackin' view of the River Medway, drapes and all trimmings. I lost all the pictures somewhere, so descriptions are vague. Although we suspect we know who upgraded us we will never know for sure.

The evening would have been unexceptional, although rather good for the most part, except for one thing which I will get to. We all had our tables allocated and sat to eat and watch the presentations, which I thought were too brief; apparently, this was a reaction to the year before, which I hadn't gone to, but were generally considered too long. The food wasn't fantastic, although as I remember the pork scratchings were to die for.

Gillian being the much more sociable animal than I would vanish off and return and I got to settle down and watch the band. They were rather good, not my usual thing, a four piece brass band with a drummer. They played their own versions of well-known tunes which was pretty cool in itself, but shortly after they had started they got off the stage and continued to play intermingling with the crowd. There was this huge throng, ball goers and the band whirling and dancing in an almost bizarre melee, it was almost hypnotic. A bit like a Baz Luhrmann movie, you know Romeo and Juliet or Moulon Rouge. Me I was still in the early stages of Gillians, "I will make a social animal of 'im or die trying' campaign, so I sat watching, playing 'air' drums quite happily.

Eventually the evening drew to an end and nothing untoward had happened, but there was still time....

Three ladies came to us to say goodbye at the end, two I knew and as I had been instructed, I leant in and kissed them on the cheek to say goodbye. This is starting to become more natural to me, but I still forget from time to time, or sometimes just don't for no reason that makes sense.

So I didn't to the lady I didn't know. I was very drunk and could offer many excuses, but probably just didn't have the bottle. I have been a social leper for years and come from a family that just don't hug or cuddle or even kiss at all really. I've often watched people who readily greet each other with a kiss or a hug and been insanely jealous. I want too but just can't. I am now starting to get there, but we're almost a couple of years and in and it's still very much a work in process. Anyway I 've wandered away from the plot again.

I didn't kiss this lady and Gillian picked me up on it. Instead of just laughing it off I lost the plot, completely. She managed to contain me until we got to our room and then I exploded. Unsure why I was in trouble, struggling with all these social niceties that just weren't natural, whilst probably utterly baffled by the amount of alcohol I'd imbibed. I don't know how I got into bed or anything much else from that night, although I woke early that morning, dwelling on the 'I can't do this, I can't do this!' train of thought, typically turning all this in on myself. I couldn't see how Gillian could possibly want to carry on a relationship with me after this performance. Half the hotel must have heard me. I did see a wonderful sunrise, the sun poking its head above the horizon and the sky changing colour gradually as the sun rose, but I didn't appreciate it. I didn't know what to do with myself, in bed, out of bed. Hoping Gillian would wake, and hoping she wouldn't, that may bring consequences. And it's hard. The more you focus on the negative (or positive), the bigger it gets. I'm getting better at sorting myself out now, but the techniques were unknown to me then and I just dwelt on the issues as I saw them and my behaviour on this night had become a monster.

Part of the reason is probably that as the walls I had had up for many years were coming down I was dealing with feelings I hadn't experienced in a long time. Don't get me wrong I had lost my rag before, but this was a whole new level. I've always suffered from what I call raging conscience, but this also was at a whole new level too. And as I've said, I'm a Libra.

When Gillian did wake, she was none too bright herself, she had also had a fair amount to drink as well as being on the receiving end of me last night and now she had to deal with an onslaught of a completely different type.

Amazingly, despite not being on top form she dealt with me very calmly and defused my anxiety pretty well. I have never known forgiveness of such enormity, Gillian humbles me continually.

I don't remember exact words obviously, but the content has been said more than once. 'with behaviour much less severe she has walked from many relationships before, but I am 'the one' (no cheese here please)' 'I am her work in progress.' She knows a lot of this is me dealing with my own demons and the other most important phrase is...

"Don't ever doubt me."

And how many times have I clung onto that one in times of self-doubt...

8. Recycling.

Just about anything left over can be re used. Some of it makes fantastic shelter for our animal friends.

Chimney pots not only make great planting, but tipped over will make great animal houses. You may have problems stopping the birds thieving any bedding you put in for their nests, but animals are pretty good at finding their own bedding.

Pallets can be great if filled with piping of all types, or layers of pebbles or other debris, even cut branches. You could put a layer of plastic over the top to keep the contents of your high rise bug or small mammal housing dry.

Left over plastic bottles could be filled up with garden cane sections or straws, in fact any type of tubing or combinations of. These can make great homes for bees.

Old fence posts could have holes drilled into them and solar powered lights attached to the top. Wedge nuts into the holes and you could attract woodpeckers into your garden and see your way by a night light. Wooden planks can be made into animal homes or nest boxes.

But the real gem is that not only are you making homes for the wildlife around you, you are engaging in a constructive use of your time that you can share with your family and reducing waste too!

Don't forget to collect water and compost too!

Chapter nine

On the up!

I have never known a love like this. We weren't out of the waters yet by any means, but we really did begin building in every way possible.

The next big project was at home, I'd always wanted to move the office out of the house and into the workshop. Partly so that the music room was just a music room, but also so that when I was at work, I was at work, even if I was at home.

There was also a fairly large section of virtually dead space beside the workshop. This was the direct result of next door putting in a new and straight fence a while previously. I'd always wanted to move the wall of the workshop. It was also sinking, we'd repeatedly taken the bottom off the door so that it would open and this was why. We'd even used it as a test for interview. Everybody wants to treat the symptom and never the actual problem, so it was a good test of thinking.

The project would entail replacing that wall and the roof, as well as replacing the front wall with glass and upvc, and putting in a phone line, broadband and a proper electrical supply. December was very quiet that year workwise and the timing was all good so we set about the work, it kept us going up until Christmas and beyond.

I love sitting in the office and looking out at the birds on the feeders, I probably get less done with them than without them, but sparrows are so entertaining, especially on the fat ball feeder just outside the window. We also regularly get dunnocks, robins and blackbirds, as well as great and blue tits and green finches and chaffinches. Of course we get pigeons and the odd rat and squirrel. There has even been a mouse occasionally. And the other day a starling came, never seen one of those out the back before. It's another of my 'favourite places'.

Christmas was novel mainly for the fact that it was Ross' first with parents in different places and that it was the first with Gillian. She moved in on Christmas Eve and stayed for 5 nights. It's funny, as I said Gillian gives gifts that are different and always from her unique perspective, so gift giving is always unexpected. It's funny, some of the clothes weren't my favourite and some didn't fit, but when we went to Canterbury at New Year to change them, I still ended up with pretty much the same things she had bought, just ones that fitted. And I wear them all too.

The other main memory is that we just crammed way too much into the time available. We went to Lloyds, Gillians eldest, and Troys, the middle one, we had my sisters family round for dinner, we went to Twickenham for big match seven, Harlequins vs Gloucester Rugby. That became an ordeal, we didn't go on the train because of all the works going on around London Bridge Station, so went in the van. It took 4 hours to get there, we missed all the build up to the game and the beginning. And typically Quins didn't win, but at least this time it was a draw and not a loss. I haven't seen a win in ages. And on the Monday we had the works do. All in all, exhausting.

So when Gillian announced she was going home on the Tuesday morning instead of the afternoon I was gutted. It made sense she went early otherwise she would have just been hanging around before she went and she had stuff to do, the salon was open the next day.

That night she went to see a friend, her bestie, Caroline and her car died on the way home. I was none to pleased, it had been suffering from low power for a while, she had to call out the AA to come and rescue her. Rightly or wrongly I felt she had gone home because she knew I wouldn't be happy about her making that trip in the car in the condition it was in. It was to become the subject of intense conversation on occasion and became a real 'hot potato' between us. When it refused to start after our trip to Canterbury... well you can imagine, although that turned out to be the battery because I had left the lights on, well, the van turns everything off when you turn the ignition off, but there you go!!!

She returned on the Friday for New Years Eve and the weekend. I was very glad to see her. It was an absolutely cool evening, we ate at home and then drove to the Berrie, as mentioned before. The first point of call on our planed pub crawl home. There weren't many people there at sevenish, but they had a quiz that we entered. We weren't going to be a threat to anyone, I think it was soap based and we just didn't know most of the references, although Gillian will tell you I did! Think dementias setting in! Shouldn't really joke about that. We had a couple of drinks there and then walked around the corner to the Telegraph. Joy of joys, they had a karaoke, I'll never be a great fan, but then I really didn't like them. We endured it mainly because we bumped into several people I knew and it's always good to catch up with folk you haven't seen in a while.

It then became clear that maybe Gillian's choice of footwear could have been more practical. She had boots with heels, the same one's she wore to the Ramblin' Man and marillion. They look really cool, but maybe aren't the best for long distances. They became the topic of conversation, but we were just so into the evening and each other, that it just added to the magic, especially as we went through a graveyard in the dark!

The next stop was what was then known as the Admiral Keppel, (it's since become (returned to) the Forrester), this wasn't such a hit, we waited ages to get served and the place just didn't have a good feeling feel. We drank up and moved on. We gave the Magnet and the Leather Bottle a miss and went straight to the Three Horseshoes. We nearly called in at Dels (the oracle), but didn't like to. Later discovered that we should've done, but there you are.

The Three Horseshoes had a fantastic vibe that night, everyone was just so friendly, they had a great supply of food, so we just stayed well into the New Year. They gave us all poppers and we all tried to shoot each other, it was just an awesome end to an awesome evening. We returned home and watched some Mission, fave goth rock band, until Ross returned from his party. He rolled in and quickly went upstairs, we think, so that we didn't realise how drunk he was(?)!

Strangely we, well Gillian and I were OK the next day, which was just as well because her sister Brenda and husband Den were coming for dinner.

Gillian later told me that it was New Years Eve when she came to the decision that she definitely really did want to be with me.... Forever. Very cool methinks.

The front windows were due to be fitted in January and we began making the house a fit place for Gillian to eventually live. We bought a new mattress after extensive testing at the wholesalers. It had to come in when the windows were out because we have a spiral staircase and there was no other way to get it in, so we had to make sure we got the right one, obviously. We decorated all the rooms throughout winter and spring, including the front room to be the perfect home for my centurions' helmet! We also fitted new windows in Ross' bedroom and the kitchen. They made such a difference that Ross now turns his radiator off because his room is too hot! It's amazing how having a totally decorated house reduces the dusting, so much so that because it's not a weekly task any more, we suddenly realise the place is filthy and then we have to go on a marathon occasionally.

I also joined another business networking group, little of significance about that, until later in the year, but mainly I wanted to be networking as close to home as possible. We had to move Canterbury ABC to a new venue because the Abbots Barton which had been our home since long before we took over put up its prices and we couldn't afford them. We moved to the Victoria Hotel.

We had Caroline and her then fella around for dinner over Christmas. Caroline's birthday is in January and she had been due to go to the theatre to see Mama Mia in London. For various reasons, she needed an accomplice at short notice and asked Gillian who obviously was delighted to go.

Another of the things that I'd never had to deal with before in my life up 'til then was 'girls nights out'. I'm pretty cool with it now, but back then I just didn't get it. It wasn't that I had any problem with Gillian going out, possibly just that it was something I wasn't a part of, well it's easy to see why not. Gillian actually asked me once if it was jealousy, if it was we'd have had a problem. Well it was, sort of, not of her 'going' with anyone else, but rather, as I've already explained above. I also thrive on the responses to texts and the like, well obviously if she's out on a night out she is not going to be checking her phone every five minutes. I managed to deal with this night out fairly well but there was another incident later on, you'll just have to wait for that one. One of my coping strategies, was as stated, 'never ever doubt me', I just had to focus on that.

That year was a leap year, I was convinced that Gillian would ask me to marry her, flattering myself obviously, anyway, she had booked 'something, somewhere' for Valentines night and I couldn't wait. I was going to ask her on Valentines Night, wasn't quite sure how or in what manner, but I was going to ask her. I did know that it wasn't going to be a public spectacle, I hate those, the proposed to have nowhere to back off to if they want to, so I don't think it's fair. Anyway once again, I digress.

Valentines was a Sunday that year, so we and the world went out on the Saturday, we went to Dino's Italian restaurant in Castle street in Dover. It was the continuation of a really Italian theme that was going to run and run, what with Hadrians wall and the Roman thing the year before.

Dino's is really old school, there are Cianti Flasks hanging everywhere, probably a few hundred of them up on all the ceiling joists; according to Angelo who runs the place, they don't make them any more so they will just add further to the charm of the place and various icons of Italian culture on the walls. Although there could be some improvement, Ferrari and no Ducati, criminal! And Mama still comes out to see all the guests when she's done cooking for the night, it's just lovely.

Gillian had been there many times before, but it was a first for us, the first of many visits. We were shown to our table and Gillian selected the wine, well she's far more knowledgeable when it comes to wine than me! We had a glass, and a few mouthfuls later it had completely gone to my head. Well, it does sometimes, not that I lost track of my highly un planned intent.

So, we're sitting there holding hands across the table, 'star crossed lovers' that we were and are, Gillian was chattering away, and I just said, 'Will you marry me?' She continued on and I said it again, 'will you marry me?' She paused and pointed several things that had to happen first and other practicalities, such as my divorce, so I then once again cut to the chase, "does that mean yes?' to which she pretty much said 'Yes'.

Absolutely spot on, that's it, that's all there is really, pretty much 'spot on.' It was like I'd waited all my life for this moment, it was just so right. I'd know more about that later, but for now we just have to roll with this. Another reality check, this most amazing woman, this most beautiful woman, who had been batting away in my camp for so long had consented to become my wife.

There were many practicalities to consider, but they could wait, tonight was ours. I have no idea what we ate, although we continued drinking pretty healthily, but one of the things that Angelo, (Dino's son) does is whip up an amazing soufflé, right there in front of you, over a flame, so Italian, or so it seems to me. I wasn't going to have a pudding that night but Gillian insisted, and as we know when Gillian insists, she will accept no refusal. So I had this pudding and my God, it was to die for, Absolutely amazing. We've had one every time we've been back there. At some point we ventured out into the night and sauntered back to Gillians, I was staying the night, Blitz was in the kennels and Ross was at his mothers. This was a rare occurrence, but neither of us had wanted to drive and we were going to Dover Castle the next day.

That was pretty cool too, we explored everywhere, in particular the Roman Pharos, a lighthouse that is very well preserved, the only one of two that has survived, almost intact. It was getting late, and it was bloody cold so we didn't hang about very long. The other memorable event was the crème tea, I am rather partial to a nice cream tea, so of course we had one, but Gillian knows me well enough to buy an extra scone, so that proves it, it must be love!

The practicalities, well there's always a few. Announcing our engagement would have to be put on hold, we didn't want to get to forward and we wanted the divorce to go through as quickly as possible and we didn't want anyone or anything to throw a spanner in the works. We wanted to get married on May 10th 2017, that would be the two-year anniversary of our first time out. That walk in the woods, do you remember? We knew where we wanted to get married too. We had been to the Tower House in Canterbury for what Gillian had thought was a wedding fair, but turned out to be an open day. We'd had Ross and his mate Gary with us and Gillian had got them primed with the right story, just in case. I loved the place and actually said to Gillian whilst on the visit, 'there's not a secret agenda here is there?' And she'll still tell you there wasn't, but I don't believe her. We did look at one or two other places, but none of them had it, they just weren't the right shade of...... as it were.

Did I mention, Gillian had agreed to marry me, WOW! Again...

We also needed to know and feel it was real, we had to tell someone or two. We decided to tell Ted and Lily, Gillian's Mum and Dad. Ted was ill, and not the happiest fella at that time, so we figured it would give him something to focus on. Gillian told them on the Monday and when I arrived a little later, the deed being done it was a bit superb, hugs, kisses and hand shaking and all that, all those things that I just don't do. But somebody knew, and that was very important, it was real to someone other than just us.

Gillian had been ferreting around the jewellery shops in Dover, funny thing that, and she had found a ring. A ring that she loved and was utterly convinced I would too, it had a roman feel to it she said. Hunt about there's a picture here somewhere. The ring had to be paid for and we didn't have enough money. Do you know what happened the law of attraction kicked in again.

I had inherited my father's half hunter watch. It didn't mean much to me except it was my fathers and as far as I know he never wore it. I'd got mums permission to sell it, but had never done much about it, I'd made a few tentative enquiries a while ago but interest had been poor. It was at this time that I had made another push. Interest in the watch as a whole was still low, but I found one jeweller who really wanted the chain and offered me a good price for it, and then in the space of a few days, the watch itself too. I didn't want it melted down for gold, it had been in the family for a long time and was a work of art. I had the money to pay for the ring now, and I know Dad would've approved. I didn't realise it then, but looking back thus is the law of attraction working overtime.

I also realised something else, do you remember I said I had started meditating, well I had continued, it was a very important part of my day. But more than that it was helping me get my sub conscious on line. I was no longer just wanting the future I had planned, but really starting to believe it would happen and believe it down to my inner core.

You see for the Law of Attraction to work you need to get three things in order. The first, you have to know what you want, and whilst on the surface this is easy, you have to be totally focussed on it, with no doubts at all. NO DOUBTS, I wasn't totally there, but I was really beginning to believe. Secondly, you have to ask for it, again seems easy, but if there are any doubts, you will block what you want coming. And thirdly, you have to be ready to receive it when it arrives and that can be bloody hard.

Let me put it this way, and I think it was Gillian whom gave me this analogy, but it's spot on, there's a man waiting for God, he takes a seat at the side of the road, after all it's a long road to God and he's tired. A tram comes passed and the driver says to the old man 'would you like a lift?' and the old man replies, 'No, I'm waiting for God.'

The tram driver nods and carries on his way. A while later a bus comes along and again stops, the driver asks the same question and again the old man replies with the same response. 'No, I'm waiting for God.'

Eventually a taxi pulls up and the scene is repeated. The taxi leaves. A long while later God comes shuffling along and the old man is so pleased, he says 'hello God, I am so pleased to see you, I have been waiting for ages.' And God replies, 'but I sent you a tram, a bus and a taxi and you're still here'. There are many analogies here, but you get the picture.

If I had any further doubts, well I did then, I had another example a short time later. Gillian and I went to a free marketing summit at Westernhanger Castle. The Castle is lovely, an almost medieval manor house sitting in well-manicured grounds, that is quite a popular wedding venue. The weddings take place in what I consider to be the opposite, an unpleasant marquee, with a very noisy fan. Anyway, this event was run by two people we'll just call Eric and Zelda. Zelda runs a very successful business and Eric claims to be very successful multi millionaire with lots of businesses. He is very confident and suave, with a real command of spoken language. This is the first stage of a planned client funnel. The next stage was two three-day courses costing four hundred pounds. Marketing was what I still felt I did not have a proper handle on. I signed on the dotted line. Working with these people was an exciting prospect.

Anyway, once again I've wandered off the plot. One of the people I bumped into there was Liz Almond one of my peers from the MMS course. We'd had several conversations then, but I'd never really understood what she was trying to help me understand at the time.

Anyway, she asked me how it was all going and I'd replied, 'well, slowly at the moment', I replied.

Her response, 'are you blocking?'

'No', I said, 'I don't think so.' Whilst I then thought 'am I?', certainly I had been focussing on the lack of work rather than actually doing much about it. What was weird, at first, was that having realised I had been focussing on the lack of work that was what I had got, when I opened up and stopped blocking the phone rang three times that afternoon. You might like to say 'ahh, that's just coincidence', but how many coincidences stop them being coincidences? I was beginning to believe that you really just have to believe.

Anyway, I now had a bit of juggling to do to go on these courses I'd just paid for. Being with Gillian means our calendar is pretty full up, not just with social events, but charitable ones and wedding fairs and the like. One I never got to, more on that later, but I did get to the Millionaire Marketing Strategy in Chatham the next month. There was a lot of good info here, mainly from Zelda, but lots to write down and think about.

That day Dale (Gillian's youngest) and Lydia had come down so that Lydia could have a dress fitting, they were getting married that summer, and then go on a girls' night out. Obviously, Dale wasn't invited to either. He came over to me and we watched a movie, Avatar I think it was, I had just bought the extended version, the evening was cool and when the movie finished he took off to join the end of the girls' night out and stay with Lydia at Gillians.

Now do you remember I said I was struggling a bit with Girls nights out, well I had that one sorted, but not the response to my messages, or the lack of response. Gillian didn't respond to some texts and I lost the plot again, anxiety kicked in, and I made a succession of stupid texts and calls. What have I done? What haven't I done? And the like, and it got to the stage where even when I got a response I still didn't sort my head out. Eventually I did get to sleep.

And when I woke up the next morning it was probably a good job I had the course to go to, it prevented me doing anything else stupid and gave me something else to focus on. As usual I was beating myself up over my behaviour. Once again Gillian put me to shame. She never threw it in my face, just my reactions to myself. 'God', she said, 'I tell everyone how wonderful you are and how much I love you and then you go and behave like that, get over yourself!'". But there was no blame, just sort it out. Her ability to forgive and move on is awesome. And how much does she love me? Again she's walked away for much less before now. It was easier when all the walls were up, but you also miss the highs, and they were just so cool.

Anyway, this course I'm on is the next stage in the client funnel for us with Eric and Zelda. The next is one to one tuition on the promise that 'if you give us ten thousand pounds we'll make you thirty'. A program we'll call 'pluto'.

I'm not overawed by Eric, but Zelda has a huge reputation. I asked her, 'is it good? Is this genuine?' and she replied, 'it's fantastic, I'm on it, we're seven weeks in and I've made seventy percent of my investment back already.' I'm interested, I have a little more than that left from mums' money which was pretty much earmarked to pay off Gillian's debts and pay for our wedding.

I call Gillian, who is dubious, but gives me the go ahead if I think it's going to be worth it. Anyway they said we get our money back if we don't make the money back. What's there to loose? I also felt Eric wanted to work with me and liked what my business did and was about. Again I signed up and awaited notification of a meeting in London which cost Five hundred quid in which we would ultimately decide to work together, this fee was also refundable.

Looking back it really was one of those where I should've followed that old chestnut of a cliché, 'if it seems too good to be true it probably is,' but it's easy to be wise in hindsight.' A colleague has since stated that it looked a really good scheme and if she'd had the money she would probably have got taken in and spent the money too.

The main thing Eric and Zelda seemed to be interested in was, what motivated me to work hard enough to make the money. Well that was easy, I was about to invest my wedding money, so I needed to make that back and I also had a fairly large mortgage for this time of my life, I wanted rid of that too. Apart from that it all appeared to be and was a done deal.

I came home and we went to Dino's for dinner. I was so fired up and so excited to be working with these people. I didn't know where we were going or what we were going to be doing but I was sure it would be exciting and push me out of my comfort zone. It felt like just the right thing at the right time. I had just left the EBC, an accountability group I had joined at the beginning of the year. It would have been better for me if I had been in one of Ash (Lawrence's) groups, but I was in one run by Sally Marshall, I like Sally, we were on the MMS together, but I didn't feel like, well there was enough accountability or ideas, so I left. I had a chat with Ash later and I think he agreed I had been put in the wrong place. He was quite happy to have me in one of his groups and I declined, temporarily at least. Looking back, I may have made the wrong decision.

Anyway, it all felt so good where I was all that time. The year was moving on and we had decided that Gillian would move in on the 15th of May. It was still all really exciting, we had our one-year anniversary on the 10th and we had been to Dino's once again. Gillian had organised a huge bunch of flowers for me. I had never had flowers before, Gillian had shown once again that you should never expect the expected from her. I was flattered. Once again, we had a lovely evening and at the end Angelo took our photo for us, we have a blown up version on the wall in our kitchen and it looks just so awesome, Gillian wasn't sure at first, but sees it now for what it is.

Sometimes I don't get me, I am doing all the lovey dovey things I never did, we talk sweet nothings all the time, hold hands all the time, repeatedly declare our love for each other, all the time. It's just not me, but it is and do you know what I love it. Stuck your fingers down your throat yet?

It was around this time that we had to have Willow put down. I had taken her on when a friend couldn't continue to give her a home. She was a labrador staff cross and had that Staffordshire bull terrier stubbornness, combined with possibly the biggest lack of intelligence I have ever met. It had taken 2 years to convince her she couldn't just clear off anytime out on a walk she felt like it, she became well trained but it had been a real battle. She did as she was told, but it was always begrudgingly. As a result I struggled to really bond or like her. Having said that she would always have a home as long as she needed it.

She had never been good at staying clean overnight, but this was just about forgivable. However, she had started to mess every time we went out, even if it was for an hour. The habit was becoming established and she was extremely hard to train on any level. It was with a heavy heart that we decided she would have to be put down. I talked to the fella we got her from, he couldn't think of any other way either. He did though help put things in context; she had come from Battersea Dogs Home and between us she'd had eight years of life she otherwise wouldn't have had.

She couldn't be rehomed either because she attacked any other dog she met, a habit she developed after we got Blitz and we were never sure what her thinking was about that. So, ultimately the decision was reached. Even taking her to the vets was a major operation because of her behaviour.

I buried her that evening, Ross came and helped. We buried her with her favourite rug and marked the spot with flowers. Ross was upset, as was Gillian, she possibly preferred Willow of the two dogs we had. I was far more upset than I expected to be, as I had said I never really gelled with her at any point, but she had been a part of my life for quite a few years.

On the fourteenth of May Gillian and I were off to London to see the last section of Solsafirs Otta tour. They were going to play the last few dates with a string ensemble and play Otta in its entirety. It was one of those nights you just knew was going to be special before you even got there. It also helped that Gillian knew and liked the majority of the album so wasn't dreading the gig like one or two of the others she had endured 'for love.' Well that's what it's all about isn't it! I'd been to wedding fairs and even gone dancing, yep, me, dancing, get in!!!

Another night memorable for some of the lunacy we indulge in, we needed a loo and couldn't find one so ended up visiting restaurants just to find a loo, and we didn't even eat in the one with the loo we used.

The gig was awesome, one of those where you hope they might have videoed one of them, but alas no. Gillian struggled a bit in the second set of earlier stuff which can be a little shrieky, well they started off as a black metal band. I like it, but....

Gillian had announced that she wasn't going to stay that night. I thought this was odd, why delay for a night and about eight hours. As usual I'd missed the obvious. She really liked her flat, she'd enjoyed her life there. Doing the things that she liked to do her way, and the freedom she had with that. Moving in with me was much bigger a deal for her than it was for me. She wanted to say good bye to her old life and her flat quietly by herself. Looking back now it is obvious, especially as I hadn't realised how much hard work it would be for us learning how to live together, as when you get to a certain age, you have gotten into set patterns and need to adjust. Again, harder for Gillian in many ways as I am very stuck in the mud, but I think we're getting there now. I think Gillian is slowly actually beginning to feel this house is her home.

Anyway, back to the plot. I dropped her off in the middle of the night and went home and to bed. As usual I slept well. When I woke up I waited for Gillian to call, she didn't let me wait too long. We loaded the van and I left her to say goodbye. Then we had a couple of calls to make before we went to ours and began sorting out all her bits and pieces.

I was on cloud nine, Gillian was, but I think was a little more aware of the challenges that lay ahead. None though as big as some we'd already dealt with.

This wonderful beautiful woman who had consented to be my wife had moved in!

The Design Bit

9. Animal, insect and bird houses. Hints and tips.

Nesting boxes come in various shapes and sizes. Tit boxes have small holes, Tits are small, but be careful wood peckers will make the holes bigger and then the tits won't use them. You can purchase boxes with metal rings, or washers to stop this happening. Robin boxes tend to have much larger openings. Half the front! Martins have mud houses which can be purchased. As we said though they must face south east or they will stay abandoned. Leave a bowl of damp mud near the nest, this will help the birds decide this is the nest for them because they will have to use less energy in making the nest suitable. You can even buy bricks now with martin nests built in!

Incidentally 61 wrens were found over wintering in one nest box once.

There are also bat boxes. It's so cool to watch bats flying in the summer from your own bat box, but they need somewhere to roost too and with the modern fascination with sealing everything up, and rightly so, we must conserve energy, a bat box would become very welcome. These are the boxes with the opening at the bottom, bats like to roost upside down.

Hedgehog homes should be somewhere secluded and face away from the north, no one wants a gale blowing in through the front door from there. And hedgehogs like to collect their own

135

The Design Bit (cont.)

bedding so leave them to it. Don't forget, they need to be able to get into your garden, a five-star hedgehog home is no use unless a hedgehog can find it! And you need to tell your neighbours too, hedgehogs need nearly 2 kilometers a night to roam in. Maybe you should invite them round for a bar be que to discuss it, in your newly designed garden, obviously!

Insect houses and tubes should face into the sun.

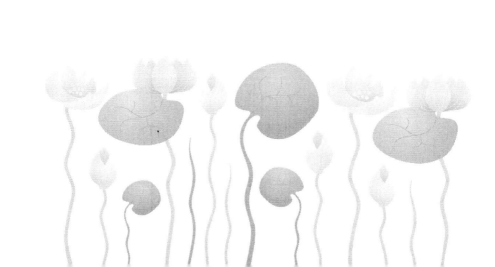

Chapter ten

May to June 2016
'Pluto' and the Butchers and Harry too.

By this time, I had completed my first design plans and was very chuffed when they got commissioned. I was surprised how keen people were to pay for my designs up front, usually within hours of receiving the invoice. This was just so cool.

Happiness was seriously setting in too. As we grow up we are told if we work hard and progress up the career ladder then we'll be happy, and as I've read and been told, and now experienced, it's the other way round. If you're happy it's much easier to gain reward because happiness is infectious and this is true for all works of life. Be happy first, then you'll enjoy working and work quite possibly won't feel like work. I certainly never have that Sunday night feeling, I love what I do to earn a living.

Doesn't stop the old way of life intruding from time to time though. We were going up to Dales that Easter to join all the Smissens on what appeared to be an annual pilgrimage. The spring had been an onslaught and I was knackered and so ready for a rest. We received an E mail from a client we had done a lot of work for a year or so previously, showing a piece of work we had done and claiming we hadn't done it properly. We knew what we had done and just knew we hadn't left it as it appeared. The e mail came so close to departure there was nothing we could do about it until we came home after Easter. Needless to say, it played on my mind all weekend and took the edge of the break that I so desperately needed. Didn't have the strategies to deal with it then! Turned out there was nothing to do or answer, relations with these clients are still good. Imaginations a bugger!

Due to issues with sub-contractors and illness we had to postpone that first commission, but another project had been approved and we began work on that before returning to the first. It was for some clients we'll call the Butchers, Mrs Butcher I had meet through networking. She seemed nice enough, on my second visit I met her husband too, he'd had cancer but was recovering well so that was cool. The plan was agreed and we proceeded to carry out the project.

The weekend before work commenced was Gillian's fiftieth birthday weekend, I had been planning this for a fair while, I knew one or two items to put on the agenda but we had some open space too. We had a room in a pleasant little hotel in Paddington. Not overly flash, but a great base to sightsee from and besides there were one or two other expensive things to do. On our first night we went to see Wicked in the Apollo Victoria Theatre. A London theatre show is always awesome, I don't see many because I'm a bit of a gig goer, but I do love 'em. Gillian had seen the show on Broadway, so knew it would be good and I was up for it because I knew she was up for it, and we couldn't find another show we both wanted to see as much. I even threw over a Steve Vai gig for it and as anyone who knows me knows, that is no small thing...

We even had dinner in a South African restaurant and you don't do that every day.

We had wanted to do one of those land and river trips with cream teas and the like, but they were all sold out. The perils of not planning everything, but not to be disheartened, we came up with the next best thing. We wandered along the River Thames for a while and found a nice spot for a cuppa whilst we made our plans. We still wanted to go on land and river trip so we booked to go on the River Duck, an amphibious vehicle from WWII. This was quite fun but would have been better but for these German kids whom complained about everything, including the fact that we had the plastic window up and they were getting splashed. The crème tea bit we did in one of those posh 'London cafes', we didn't mind paying a lot if what we got was worth it. On this occasion it wasn't. The trays had obviously been made during the morning, and then left on display. As a result the two end sandwiches had become a little dry, so we asked if they could be changed. Well this wasn't a cheap afternoon tea. The request wasn't greeted warmly and the replacement sandwiches, when they did arrive were I think the result of two more end sandwiches replacing the two moist sides. As you can imagine we were well impressed. We walked back to the hotel across Kensington Park which was pleasant, if a little longer than Gillian would've liked. I keep forgetting that what is a gentle stroll for me is a route march for her, especially with inappropriate footwear!

We were still having difficulties finding an operative to work alongside Ash, our last temporary employee had let us down the Friday before. We knew he had a job coming, but had expected a little more notice.

So, sitting on a bench in Green Park in London I am making phone calls to try and keep staffing levels as needed for Monday. Eventually I spoke to a friend of Gillians who had an unemployed partner, he agreed to help us out for a couple of days. Relief, which was short lived. He didn't last two hours before he left, without a word. He never did call me and apologise, or even let me know. That kind of behaviour annoys me, at least have the decency to let me know you can't do it. It was Ash who called me with the news.

It's at this point that we prepare for the main event of the London trip. I have booked us a table at the Shard and we move into another world completely.

The Shard, I've been passed it on the train many times but never thought much about it. It's a big glass structure that has a restaurant at the top. A place where people unlike me go, I'm not even sure I'm that keen on the look of it, but Gillian wants to go there on her birthday. So, I had to sort it. You can only book three months in advance so that was infuriating. I'd wanted the whole weekend sorted as soon as possible. I'd looked at the menu, then when I'd decoded it and seen the prices, I had to pick myself up off the floor. But this was what Gillian wanted so I had to make it happen. Gillian had given me one of those money boxes that you can only open with a hammer and I had been saving since my birthday the year before. It's amazing how much you can save without realising it, especially when you put every pound coin you get in there. I was even spending notes when I had the change just to get more pound coins.

When we smashed it a couple of nights before we left, there was enough to pay for the evening, probably. Wooo...

After we had eventually found our way in, well we are country yokels, well I am, and emerged into the restaurant the first thing that hits you is the noise, it's loud, so much conversation. A mixture of awe and is it going to be this loud all evening? But the service, the service in a place like this is superb, totally unlike the place we went to in the afternoon that by now didn't exist. A waiter approached us and showed us to the bar, he sorted the wine list for us. I put the responsibility for that straight to Gillian. She chose what to us was a very expensive Malbec, but in Shard terms was at the lower end of the scale.

A short time later we are collected and taken to our table. There are tables all around the Shard, some near the centre of the restaurant and some in the middle, and then there are the tables right at the edge, by the enormous glass windows. The gentleman has asked us to follow him and we're quietly hoping for one by the glass, not believing it's possible. But it is, man how cool is this, we're right by the glass, right by the glass, and the view over London is spectacular. It's so hard to take it all in. Where to look, even just sitting down and looking normal is hard. To many this must be the norm but to us it's another world, one that at the moment we get to dip our toes into, but it is going to become our norm too. Thankfully it's much quieter here.

I'd booked our table for eight o'clock, well if you're going to go to the Shard with a view like that it would be criminal not to be able to watch the sunset over London and we did. Like the yokels I described we took photos and videos, had our photos taken, the waiters are used to it and even know how to get the best with all light and all angles. This had to be one of the best sunsets I've ever seen.

And did I forget to mention I was with Gillian, my Gillian, who looked stunning tonight. I'm a bloke so I can't remember what she wore and I'm not going to wax any more lyrical, you'll have to get over it. But none of this would have mattered one jot without her.

The wine she chose was beautiful, a really fantastic red, and it was putting a lovely blur around the edges. It didn't though dull our taste buds, I can't remember what we had as a starter, but I had pork for main and Gillian had the beef. I have never tasted food the like of which before, stunning, so good you don't want to chew, just make the eating last forever. Perfect time to really get into a spot of mindfulness meditation, well, should you remember that is. We had a chat about how to proceed after the main course and decided that although we could have a pudding and then tea and coffee, if we added all that together it came to..... a....... bottle of...... wine. Do you know what we chose? Yes, you do.

You only get a table for two hours, so the beauty of an eight o'clock booking is that you don't have to leave and we wanted to savour this experience for as long as possible. And we didn't leave until we were ready. Well as Rob (Smith of Cure fame) said, 'on a night like this...'

Well we might have had to descend, but we were still very high. One of the best nights of certainly my, but probably our lives, I'm not quite as cosmopolitan as Gillian, but we're working on that.

We returned on the Saturday in time for the family celebration of Gillian's fiftieth, day three of the festivities and why not. But we had an extra especial motive for this one, you see we had got the all clear on the divorce and that meant we could let our proverbial cat out of the bag. Great to share the news with the world and great not to be keeping a secret. All the close members of her family were there, the three boys Lloyd, Troy and Dale and their respective families as well as Ted and Lily, her mum and dad.

Gillian made the announcement, there was a moment pause after which Troy stated, 'Yeah, I'm really pleased about that!' There then followed the expected rounds of congratulations. We were fairly confident that our decision would be approved of, but to have our faith rewarded was superb. The boys after all had been Gillian's 'idiot filter' for many years. And Troy is possibly the ring leader. What did he do then, took Lloyd off to the local store and came back with alcohol for everyone (that wanted it). Very Troy.

We had wondered when we told Ted and Lily whether Ted would manage to keep the news a secret. Not you understand from any desire to tell, but we wondered if he'd let it slip inadvertently. There was just the one occasion when potential disaster was missed rather than averted.

It was a big secret to keep and Ted so wanted to share it, there was one occasion when the proverbial cat nearly got out of said bag...

He suffering with emphysema and heart problems and was in Canterbury Hospital getting treatment for the problems caused by water retention in his legs when we went to visit him. His condition was becoming serious so we'd taken Lloyd and Emily with us to see him. When we'd got there Ted was in bed and not terribly happy with his care. He'd just signed a DNR (do not resuscitate). This had unsettled him and made the realty of his illness more apparent. Thus, he chose this day to give me his blessing to marry Gillian; although he'd approved our marriage he hadn't actually said as much to me directly. His actual words were fairly straight, 'I'm giving you my blessing for that thing we've discussed. I've seen how you are with the girls, Emily and Orla, and Gillians boys. I want you to take my place when I'm gone.' My God, this was a seal of approval I had totally not expected and once again I'm humbled. I may overuse the word, but you can see why. I absolutely love this family that I'm becoming a part of.

Lloyd was in clear earshot, but appeared to miss the news, although surely a bell must've rung somewhere. Especially when Ted reached out his hand for me to shake. A big thing for Ted and not to be rebuked at all! When we left the hospital I was holding back the tears

Gillian's birthday was becoming a blur of awesome times and celebration on more than just one theme. On the Sunday she had her public birthday, a bit like the Queen. And Gillian, being Gillian, couldn't pass up on the opportunity to raise much needed cash for the Harmony Therapy Trust, decided to turn the event into a fund raiser for the charity. We had bands, a bar-b-que, raffles and food and the like. The barn, did I mention it was held in the Thatched Barn at Farthingloe, just outside Dover run by Gill and Colin

The Barn is a fantastic old building that is, well, thatched. It nestles into the hillside just of the road, well a long road, so not only is the barn itself pretty evocative, but it's setting is also pretty spectacular. As you drive along the entrance way the barn appears, the thatch first then the wooden walls. When you enter the light leaves and you enter an atmospheric semi darkness. As your eyes adjust you take in the amazing woodwork that supports the thatch and take in the surroundings. The barn is on two levels, with light coming in from windows at either end. Oh, and there is a bar!

The most important part, obviously Gillians speech thanking all those who had come and all about the trust and the activities still to happen, and she also used the event to publicly announce our engagement. I had stayed out of the way, after all this was Gillian's show, and couldn't get to her at that time, but that was kinda cool too. We are very supportive of each other and as I said this was her day. It did feel good to be public though and Gillian had hated having her engagement ring and not be able to wear it!

What a four days, and what a way to celebrate a major birthday.

The next day we began the next major project, the garden renovation for the Butchers. As I said before, Ash spent the majority of the day on his own and once again I was back on the phone. Another of the good folk I got to know was Chris. Chris was Polish, he had come to this country for work. And work he could. He was available and came on site the next day. His work ethic was superb, as was the quality of his work. He was a real asset to the project. We were very grateful to him for his efforts, so motivated to the cause was he that when he fell behind the pace he expected of himself, he bought in a colleague at no extra charge. We did make a contribution for him though.

We had several difficulties with the weather, so the work took a little longer than I had expected. The Butchers, unknown to us at the time weren't happy about this, we had also had to deal with getting differing information for either of them. Occasionally we weren't sure what they wanted, we always try to follow a policy of the client is always right, but sometimes it's difficult. One example, paint the sleepers, don't paint the sleepers, and painting the sleepers wasn't even in the job description, but if we can help out we always will, after all we want our clients to have what they want, if at all possible, and if we can do it at no extra cost then we will.

On the second Wednesday I arrived on site and saw the artificial turf that Ash and Chris had laid. I was impressed and thought they had done a fantastic job, so was a little surprised when Mr Butcher very politely, but aggressively told me it was the worst laying of turf he'd ever seen. As I said I was very impressed with the work, if seen several and we've lain a few and it was good. We looked at a few on you tube, yes there was better, but the majority were not. We met in the middle on that one and I thought that issue had been put to bed.

I shot a vlog of the nearly finished garden, showed it to Mrs Butcher who approved it and I duly posted it on Facebook. Mrs Butcher liked it, her mother liked it and her mother in law liked it too. There were also favourable comments posted as well. It was a good day.

I finished the project on the Friday with Harry. It was raining so we couldn't finish all the tasks and explained all this to Mrs Butcher before I asked her to sign the job off as we always do, as a matter of policy.

This she did, and Harry and I left pleased with what we believed, and still believed to be a job well done.

Before we got home we had a call from Mrs Butcher to say that actually she wasn't happy at all. I arranged to go back on the Monday and address any concerns she might have. Nothing major, but the client has to come first. We would've called the next week anyway, again it's a matter of policy.

So as you can imagine I was somewhat shocked and surprised on the Saturday when I opened my e mails to discover an E mail from Mr Butcher that was nearly two pages long outlining how he had returned home to find his wife upset and devastated and outlining a long list of issues he had with the work and the work we had done. One thing was for sure he had certainly put a lot of work into the construction of this E mail. On face value it was horrific, except that we are a very process lead business and have procedures that we follow very carefully, and Mrs Butcher had signed off the job willingly, we had even joked about coming back later in the year to see how the planting had grown.

As you'll be aware we had made a great effort after our past to make sure that this kind of thing couldn't happen again. Mrs Butcher knew all about this because I had done a presentation about all these events at the network meeting. I make no claims here.

I spoke to Eric on the Tuesday, hoping he would have some way of dealing with the situation in a way unknown to me. But he knew no more than I, should have suspected another drama brewing right there, anyway that's another story.

So, what to do? We had to meet them, you can't sort out conflict without discussion, but there had been several examples of U turns within the Butcher camp that I was unsure how this would turn out. Gillian suggested I ask her good friend Collete to come along. And she agreed to, that was a relief. An observer.

As the smoke cleared we met in the Butchers kitchen on the Friday. To be fair all was very civilised, cases put and defended by both sides. We made an agreement very successfully too, which Collette made sure was clearly understood by everybody.

We would remove all the planting and remove the cost of the planting from the bill. I was happy with that and Ash duly removed the planting as instructed. We all left feeling we had sorted a difficult situation. Thanked Collete and dropped her home.

We supplied the revised invoice on the following Monday, even supplying a copy of all the receipts so no duplicity could be inferred and do you know what? Yeah, you do, they refused to pay it! And made a pathetic offer instead...

I was pretty damned sure that if we'd taken them to court we would've won, after all we had a signed off jobsheet, we had the facebook post with the video and the comments that had occurred, and we had a witnessed agreement that they had reneged on.

However, that all had to be weighed up against the negativity that would surround us, the bad PR that would have gone up on social media, and you can imagine how they may have used the cancer issue to their advantage. He had certainly stated that I had no understanding about these long and debilitating illnesses, I certainly wasn't going to talk to him about Ted, or, my mother. He made other unfounded assumptions too, such as Harry being on 'community service', which was totally not the case.

I have to say I have fallen out with clients and understood their complaints even if I don't agree with them, but I've never felt played before and this time I felt played. These were not nice people.

Going to court was just not worth the effort or the negativity for the amount of money they wanted to save.

Ultimately though the beauty of this was that we had a policy as to how we should deal with these situations, we tweaked it a little afterwards but we knew what to do and how to behave. This meant we were in a much stronger position to negotiate. It wasn't the result we wanted, but we had handled the situation well and could hold our heads up high.

I guess at this point we should say a few words about Harry. Harry joined us via a program designed to help kids that struggled to succeed with our education system get, at the least, a reference, or more preferably an apprenticeship. Harry wanted to work, that was a major plus, but for him the real icing on the proverbial cake was that he got on with Ash, and Ash had tolerated the last few potential employees. So when his free time came to an end I was more than happy to take him on.

Ash will say, 'come on Harry,' and turn and walk away and Harry will fall in a step behind, so I call them Winnie the Pooh and Piglet!

I was also beginning to have serious doubts about 'pluto', I voiced these to Eric, but as a master of 'owning the conversation' as he calls it I felt the fault was all mine by the end of it and I had to change. Thing is, having done the MMS, there was nothing I was being told or asked to do that I didn't already know, this was starting to look like an expensive waste of money. I voiced my concerns to Zelda on a regular basis, but nothing was changing.

I'd also had a week with three presentations in it and Eric had asked me to go to see him in London and he would go through my presentation with me so I would know who to turn it into a money spinner. Basically, this consisted of removing all the interesting info and stating, 'within the business we have the knowledge to help you with this.' Which turned out to be rubbish, really rubbish. I'd always felt that at some point in time Eric would start really delivering the goods, give me something to really get my teeth into, because most of his conversation is empty. As I said, I bought into Zelda not him.

It never happened. Anyway, I tried to do the talks as he instructed, feeling well if he's done it, it must be right. Not so. It was boring for me, and I presume boring for the listeners too. I wasn't long before I went back to my tried and trusted methods and the very next meeting I got one gardens rounds client and one new lead.

I did a presentation to the network September, it was a visitors day, so the room was packed. Colette had even come in her capacity as a marketer for Dover. I imagine Mrs Butchers jaw dropped a little when she saw her. I did a presentation about the law of attraction. It's always interesting to see people's reactions to that content, but as you will be aware it is now a huge part of my life, so I believe in it passionately. Anyway Collete was watching Mrs Butcher and found her behaviour to be extremely odd, don't know how many people may have thought the same.

I continued with the network until my subscription ran out, but as no other work came my way, (and I know how to network) there was no point in renewing.

In the June that year Ted died. We had been to see him on the Sunday. When we said goodbye on that day I felt it was probably the last time I would see him alive, I think he knew it too. It was just there in the conversation.

He passed away quietly on the Tuesday. When I got the call from Gillian I knew what had happened.

He and Lily had a friend around and had been chatting in the kitchen. Feeling tired, he'd decided to go back to the living room for a nap and whilst asleep he had passed away. I think he would have liked that too, I imagine he'd been able to hear the voices of Lily and their friend in the kitchen as they softly chatted away.

As with my mother, he, I'm sure, had figured the time right, for him personally, life would have become much more difficult from this point, the onset of emphysema was likely to increase greatly, that combined with the fact he knew Gillian would be alright now, not only did he know we were going to get married but we were able to share our news now. Dale was about to get married and he knew he wouldn't be able to go to the wedding. Troy and Lloyd were settled with their families and Brenda (Gillians sister) and her family were long settled. But I think he was really happy that Gillian was finally settled, as I said he made quite a thing of giving me his blessing. Cool fella was Ted!

A couple of weeks later was the funeral at Barham. I was most surprised to be asked to speak at the ceremony. I had only known Ted for just over a year, so it was just unreal to be asked to speak, as I said (written that a lot lately) I absolutely love this family I am marrying into. I was also relieved when so many people came up after and said how eloquently I had spoken. Lily told me she thought I had got it about right. Phew. Afterwards we had the wake and a very private party at home later. That was cool too.

We all miss Ted, his love of family, and of course, stories was unparalleled.

10. First thoughts about planting.

There are many considerations to think about when planting, first where in your garden are you actually planting?

You need to think, kind of laterally when planning planting, you should begin with any walls or fencing in the garden and work towards the paths or main vantage points, reducing plants in height or width as they approach your main viewing area. Another way is to triangulate the area you are looking at, this will vary the height of the horizon.

Colour can be important, do you want a singular colour theme in your garden, or have two contrasting colours. Bright colours can appear to reduce garden size and less imposing flowering can give a greater impression of size.

Purple is the colour seen most clearly by bees, foxgloves are another favourite, but think about the year round too, bluebells, hardy geraniums and penstemon will keep the bees in your garden and as the year progresses so will hebes, buddlieas and fuschias.

If you use indigenous plants, that is plants that are native to the location then they will be well suited to the soil and other local conditions, and our indigenous wildlife will have the food source it needs. Plants have varying degrees of tolerance for their environment, for example some like it wet, some moist and some dry! The soil type you have will determine the colour of flowers you get if you have a hydrangea. And obviously some plants prefer brighter sunlight than others which are shade loving!

And then, when planning planting, start from the borders and work inwards.

A hedge is a fantastic border, but can take up a lot of space.

If you have fencing then you may want a climbing plant to cover or hide it. Ivy looks fantastic, is good for our wild friends, but can be very invasive and destructive, thus requiring more maintenance than other planting. Wisteria looks fantastic but once again, when established grows very quickly. Both are labour intensive but worth it

Virginia creeper provides shelter and cover for birds and insects, attaches itself with suckers and requires less maintenance, and when the leaves turn brown in the autumn they are beautiful.

Honey suckle is fantastic, but make sure you get a creeper because not all cover acreage. Clematis is another great climber and some of the flowers are awesome. Passion flowers are awesome too, the flowers are spectacular and on a south facing wall can flower from early summer right into autumn. And don't forget wild roses are pretty spectacular too!

The Design Bit (cont.)

In front of these borders place buddleia and verbena or perennial wallflower, fantastic for butterflies, the former is known as the butterfly bush. And for obvious reasons, peacocks (butterflies, not the birds) love it!

We spend a lot of time talking to the owners of the plant nursery we use to make sure we get just the right plants for the garden. Always check with people who know more than you do, they will always be pleased to help out!

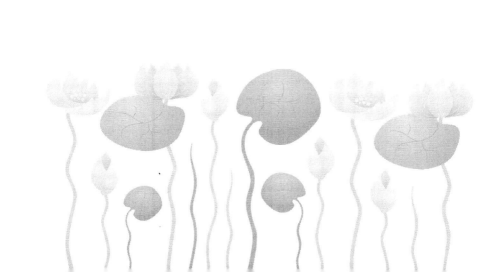

Chapter eleven

The Ridgeway pivotal. Ready to fly.

You may recall, right back at the beginning I started off talking about the West Highland Way. The next few years featured several long distance walks. I also talked a lot about Hadrians Wall Path (HWP). We also walked the North downs Way (NDW), or accidentally fell into it. That was possibly the hardest walk we did, albeit not because the walk was tough, but again that's a story for another time.

This year, we walked the Ridgeway. We set about this one differently to the way we had done the last few. The HWP was fantastic, but it had become clear that this aging body was struggling to walk these distances with my world on my back, we either did shorter distances and therefore take longer or we carry less. We also wanted a little time on the walk not walking. Ultimately we only had a week, so taking longer wasn't an option. Ross and I decided to use B and B's this time and just carry clothing and food. This meant that Blitz would also have to stay at home.

Anyway, once again I'm getting ahead of myself. We left on the Friday for Dales Wedding on the Saturday, with Ross and Lloyd in the back, to struggle with seats that had no leg room, Lloyds family were with Troy. I didn't realise it at the time, but one of the elements of the walk started on this journey. Ross and Lloyd were playing Pokemon Go. We were going so slowly along the M25 that they were able to hatch eggs, or something. But it was funny to hear the cries of distress when the traffic did pick up the pace and these eggs then refused to hatch!!

Ross and I would begin the walk on the Sunday after the wedding.

That evening nearly all the males from both families took to the Bald Buzzard in Leighton Buzzard for a few beers and yes the comparison has been made. It was a really enjoyable evening, but it was obviously noticeable that there was a large amount of restraint in the air. We all wanted a few beers, but we also all knew that there could be no hangovers of consequence the next day. But it was so cool that Ross and his future step brothers were getting on really well. Troy is currently helping Ross with his best man duties.

Saturday dawned and we had to be up reasonably early, Gillian was on hair and make up duties, after all this is what she does. She vanished and Ross and I helped set up the marquee and the wicker path and the like.

I was on duty as dress monitor and fitter for when Gillian had finished with all the bridal party. When the message reached me I had to be dressed and in attendance to get Gillian in to her dress, it had a corset like fitting on the back. This I had never done before, but had watched a couple of you tube videos. Seemed simple, what could go wrong? Pretty much nothing, but considering Gillian was trying to do her hair as I got her into her dress and was moving around the room, it was a bit difficult. There was a slight kink at the bottom, but I photo'd my handiwork to show her I was proud and that she could be seen in public. It had been a bit of carry on but we succeeded, with literally minutes to spare.

The service was in a small village church and very traditional in every sense. There were a few photos after the service, but for the most part, we all moved onto Pete and Lisa's, (Lydia's mum and dad) where the reception was being held, for the rest of the day.

Dale and Lydia entered through a confetti strewn corridor of guests and all had a glass of the bubbly stuff. The afternoon was just about as right as you could wish for. There was no rush for anything at all, we just had just the right amount of sun giving just the right amount of heat, there was just the right amount of space and seating for everyone to stretch out and enjoy the afternoon. The photographer, Alexa, was floating about just capturing the afternoon and I have to say she did an awesome job too. There was a magician keeping children of all ages amused and waiters and waitress with drinks and nibbles who generally managed to appear just when you felt their services were required.

Gillian was doing the rounds as she loves, especially in her capacity as Mother of the Groom, sometimes just watching her happy and in her element from a distance is just so cool. There if needed but giving her space when she needs it too. I spent much of the afternoon chilling with Ross on a sun lounger thing that rocked back and forwards drinking champagne and eating canapés, very decadent.

Eventually we all made our way into the marque for the meal and speeches. How cool it is to have a garden big enough to hold a marque for your Daughter's Wedding!

I was most honoured that Dale and Lydia had wanted me to sit with Gillian on the top table, have I mentioned that this branch of the Smissens are a cool lot. But I hope it's as obvious to the rest of the world as it is to us, Gillian and I are madly, sickeningly in love. Said it again, get me. Anyway, as I said I was most chuffed to be asked to sit on the top table and even more bowled over when I got a gift too, a crackin' engraved tankard. I know the wedding was not about us, but we have some fantastic photos where we look, because we are, so happy.

Dale had been a little worried about his speech, but was superb and more than a match for his new father in law. Eventually the evening progressed and the band came on. Dale and Lydia had obviously practised their first dance well and performed like the stars they were on the day. Gillian had made it her match to fill the wishing tree with good wishes so was all over the marque, keeping an eye on her was difficult, but it was so cool to be able to appear when needed. Not you understand that I am possessive or a stalker, but we love to look out for each other and one of us always manages to stay sober enough for when the other one needs us too, which is also, just so cool.

Eventually all good things, as they do, must come to an end and we were just about the last to leave, I can remember waiting by the village green for our taxi to take us back to the hotel.

The next morning we were far healthier than we had any right to be. We made our way down to the restaurant for our last breakfast together for a week. Gillian was going to take Ross and I to Ivinghoe Beacon so we could begin walking the Ridgeway. It's a mixed feeling you know, I was really looking forward to spending a weeks quality time with my son and walking long distance walks is a fantastic way to spend some active R and R, and see new places. But I wouldn't see Gillian for a week and I was going to miss her. It was only a short way from the hotel. Gillian took our photos before returning to Pete and Lisa's for a bar-be-que before she returned home and a week of mostly work.

Ivinghoe Beacon is high up on the downs and has commanding views for miles and miles all around. It's all rolling hills as far as the eye can see. Real big sky country. The kind of place you might expect to see buzzards or red kites in the sky, but not today. We did well on the first day, managing to get a little lost within ten minutes of leaving the beacon.

We were keen to get the pacing better on this walk, and for the most part we succeeded, the first couple of days were long, but this was so we could ease the pace as the walk went on. We stayed in some fabulous places, the Red Lion in Wendover, lovely room in purple with a bath. Orchard Cottage on the next night, greeted with a cream tea and then ferried to and from the pub because it was raining, a youth hostel, and then the Court Hill Centre.

The Court Hill Centre is fairly large, an old building surrounding a courtyard, I think originally it had been stables but now is converted into an outdoor centre, we understand it is very popular as a base for school visits and activity holidays, but when we visited there it was just us and a family of Dutch folk. The views were fantastic from the top of the ridgeway generally, but especially here at the centre. There was nowhere nearby to go and get a meal so we cooked for ourselves and then chilled as we wished. It was lovely to spend some time with Ross doing what he wanted to do, we spent an hour playing football in our stocking feet until my knee said, 'do you want to walk tomorrow?' We explored the inside of the place and played cards, just spending quality time together, which can be difficult with a teenager. We even had a fairly long conversation.

The next day we moved onto see the White Horse of Uffington and Uffington Castle and whilst they were spectacular there was a more eerie place. We found a copse that had an old military pill box in it. It definitely appeared to be lived in by someone at some time, it was not clear if it was currently occupied or not. We didn't like to go in, they weren't very tidy, but there were offerings all over the place, almost like a pagan ritual, you know flowers and carvings and even a few inscriptions. There was definitely a sense of something.

We then stayed in the thatched Chaney Thatch, a beautiful old building that was still in the early nineteen hundreds in many ways, reminded of my Grans when I was a kid. The owner was an eccentric lady who had flown planes and ran re unions for people who flew certain aircraft. Ross was definitely her favourite, I was routinely ignored, not that it mattered. Half the fun of walking is the people you meet.

The whole walk was dominated by Ross playing Pokeman Go and regularly vanishing and charging off to go and get this 'item' or do battle with something. I'm not entirely sure what it was all about, but if it gets youngsters out into the countryside then it has to be a good thing. Ross was even having a battle with somebody around Uffington Castle. They would battle him and get something, and then he would steal it back. It was quite entertaining; I think he lost in the end.

There were two very important realisations for me on this trip and they both have to do with this thing called the law of attraction that you might have heard me babbling on about from time to time. The first was the pair of binoculars we found. Because when we were packing we were focussing on Dales wedding just as much as walking I had overlooked my binoculars. And for me that is a major disaster. I just know if I haven't got my binoculars the most fantastic sighting or views of whatever will emerge, in the same way that if you haven't got your mobile phone, the car will pack up or the world will end and you won't be able to call for help or tell anybody.

So, on the third day, funnily the first day that had some fantastic views since the first day, we were walking through some very open land when Ross cried out, 'Dad, Look!" and ran over to a gate where there were some binoculars. We could see for miles around and there was nobody anywhere so they hadn't been left recently. I was a little conflicted as to whether we should take them, but ultimately, we did. If anyone we met had asked us I would have given them up, but no one did. I was so chuffed, the countryman naturalist in me was complete once more. The law of Attraction had provided me with what I needed right when I needed it, obviously just another coincidence. No way, there have been just too many of them. It even works with parking spaces. The other day when I went into town I went to park in the road I generally use and the were no spaces, 'bloody law of attraction' I thought, before I then came to the three spaces that are never empty, and there was a space. You just have to have faith.

The other, well Gillian was booking the wedding venue that week and was having difficulty making contact with them, and also busy. This was important, obviously and as communications were coming through with the pace of a stoned snail I was starting to do a great job of winding myself up. I was imagining all kinds of situations and scenarios, none of them good. BUT, as I have been traveling this road to some kind of self-discovery and managing to find some inner calm I have some strategies to help me. Once again all coming from that basic of philosophies, the law of attraction. The thoughts I was focussing on were what I was attracting, obviously, and that meant they were feeding of each other, growing bigger. What I had to do was break the cycle. And how to do that, well as I said, meditate. You don't have to have crossed legs and upturned palms, you can meditate anywhere and at any time, well maybe not when driving, but you know! So, that is what I did. The idea is just to focus on the now and the breath, the mind will wander, but when you realise just bring it back to now and the breath. This is not always easy, but when I stopped dwelling on unhealthy thoughts they went away and I felt better. They would come back, but would be dealt with again. I'm not properly there yet, but compared to that Easter trip I'm a lot further along the road... Needless to say, when the message came through that the Tower House was booked and so was a meeting to confirm it all I was still mightily relieved.

It was wonderful at the end of the walk to meet up with Gillian and have a 'normal' holiday. We had a fantastic day at Kenilworth Castle, the place is largely a ruin, but still has enough of it intact to give you a feel of what the place must have been like when the Earl of Dudley lived there. It's very statuesque and monumental in size and scope. I loved it.

The Friday I think it was I went for a walk along the Thames with Gillian and it was just glorious. The sun was out, but not too hot. We walked along the river hand in hand and talked about all things, plans and ideas and sometimes just stuff. There was bridge that we went and stood on the top of and played pooh sticks. The river at that spot reminded Gillian of the Daintree River in Cape Tribulation in Australia. We returned to the path and walked to a lock. We watched the lock keeper open and shut the gates and flood the bit on the middle, I shot a video about the swallows that were gathering and put it on Facebook and we wandered around the rest of the walk and returned to the cottage before hiring a pedallo thing and being zoomed up the river by Ross, he just doesn't like to do slow at all, well, teenagers ay!

We also had John and Tam round for a bar-b-que, we see them once a year and usually when we are on holiday. John is in the Marines and they live in Devon, they were on their way to his parents in Leicester, so it just worked out right. So that was also a highlight.

On our way home, we stayed for a night with the newlyweds, recently returned from honeymoon in Paris. Whilst we were there I went snowboarding with Ross, and utterly trounced him, which annoyed him because he thought he'd really be good at it because he does a lot of skateboarding.

And then we returned home.

Now, I am almost at the end of the story...

11. Finally, the finishing touches.

Having got all the hard, landscaping, planting, animal homes and water sorted, you may feel your garden is finished, but there is one more element you must think about!

There is more of YOU that can be put into your garden. Statues, sculptures or other ornamentation can help give your garden an ethos that makes it your favourite place. You may have already included this in some of the features we have already discussed, for example water features, which can have fabulous designs and obviously animal homes. But there are statues available from any source you may feel inspired by, Greek mythology for example, here is a statue of Vergogna Phryne. But you could opt for birds, animals, fairies, gothic or even film characters. These additions can make your garden even more you!

Ultimately, get out there and dream, It's all possible!

Epilogue.

Which as I said, ultimately brings me to the end of my story, but you might have noticed there are a number of loose ends to tie up and one or two things that might need to be explained.

Firstly, why stop here? It felt like I was at almost the exact mirror image of where I was three years ago, then I was just about to begin a fantastic holiday having had been in a great place with a very promising future, totally unaware that without processes and foundations the whole lot could come crashing down at any time, which as you now know it did.

Ash is still here and Harry will have passed his apprenticeship!

Compared to now, where I have just returned from a great holiday, and the future is awesome because I won't let it be any other way, the business is utterly processed and I have strategies to deal with my own life and how I handle what happens within it.

So 'a handyman for all seasons', a successful business that was built on very shaky foundations has morphed into 'simple life' a real powerhouse of positive credibility based on solid processes; whilst you have to be prepared for the unexpected at all times, we haven't met a situation we didn't have a process to follow in the last year and a half. We are ready for anything!

I also returned from holiday with an awful lot of calls to return and ultimately these resulted in a lot of work. In fact, from that point the business has gone from strength to strength. No longer did I have to keep it afloat with mums' money, which incidentally at this time had run out.

And it also had to work well enough that not only did I get a wage, a decent wage from it, but I also had to make enough money to pay for a wedding and a honeymoon, having squandered the remaining money on what turned out to be what I consider a fraudulent investment, 'pluto'.

There are two further examples to evidence that statement, the first, I wrote Eric a long list of issues that I wasn't happy about; his response, he didn't acknowledge any of them, he just stated, 'I feel your pain'. And....

The second, I had a phone conversation with him, it was on a Thursday between meetings. At the end we had been on the phone for an hour and a half, I hadn't realised the duration, my clock is on my phone, and he had told me absolutely nothing, and I mean absolutely nothing. And I was now late for my second meeting. It was at this point I knew that this arrangement had to end. 'pluto', more like Uranus!

I had hoped he would be big enough to admit his part in why this hadn't worked, maybe even honour his statement to refund my money. For someone who doesn't do blame, all he did was point his finger at me and ultimately, alas, his communications just became abusive.

Another lesson learned.

Following intervention by the legal people we have had a meeting designed to find a solution. Working on a philosophy of something is better than nothing, they have offered us an internet package that will run through a colleague of mine. I sincerely hope it is as good as they say it is. It would be great to be able to say, 'that Eric, really cool fella he is.'

Well it would wouldn't it!

Whatever, I'm certainly not going to carry any negativity around with me. I'll make my money honestly. And incidentally, I never did go on his 'business success strategy' course.

And Zelda, well Zelda has, as a colleague stated, 'dodged the bullet'. I will probably just accept that at least I put a division between them and anyway, Karma is a bugger!

Far more importantly, by the time you read this I will have married Gillian, and I'm still kicking myself about that reality. We still have our disagreements, we are both strong willed people, Gillian has been used to making all the decisions on her behalf and I have got used to doing things my way. But as we remind each other, we just don't want to ever stop trying to get it right for each other. Opening yourself up to love is vulnerability, a trust that should never be broken or abused.

Gillian came up with another awesomely simple gem which was a gamer changer. Having once again been a plonker, although not intentionally this time, I was starting to turn it in on myself, see I'm not there yet, she said, 'sort yourself out, it's not all about you you know!' Absolutely, don't you think; misery is selfish!

We had had our engagement party on the August bank holiday that year, we had to do it in the three sections, first we had family round for cooked brunch, we then had the high society folk round for Bar-be-que number one and then those that are possibly best described as the 'pissheads' for bar-be-que number two. It was an awesome day, Gillian and I just had to pace ourselves. All comments afterwards suggest all had as much fun as we did.

And where did we host this party? Why in the garden at our house. The garden I designed to be one of my favourite places and the garden that I based the 'how to design a garden videos' around. I/we love spending time out there, often sitting under a rug when the temperatures a little chilly, there is also a section of pergola that is under cover so we can stay out there when it's raining.

One great point of note was that this was the day I asked Ross to be my best man. I was pretty sure he would be up for it, I'm sure he could see that I was so happy with Gillian and I knew he got on well with her, so when he just said 'Yes', and shook my hand which being a Pollard he never does, was just so cool.

The Ridgeway is also probably the last long distance walk I will do for a fair while, especially with Ross. At seventeen he is going on holiday next year with his mother and has plans to go on holiday with his mates too. And he is definitely not coming on our honeymoon.

My divorce finally came through in the October, although the Nationwide are still mucking us about with taking my ex-wife off the mortgage, but that will happen too.

I also appreciate you might be thinking that this law of attraction thing is just a massive mind job, and you know you might be right, but whatever it is I'll take it. It is just so cool knowing that something will 'drop in' when you need it, it removes worry from my life. And it follows that divine timing is absolutely spot on, the people and the resources always appear right when you need them.

You also need to be active and totally focussed on the things you want and put everything in place yourself, it's not just an opportunity to do nothing, because if that's all you focus on that is all you will get. It's all just easier if your happy, and success comes from happiness, not the other way round. So, if it's a nut job I'll take it. But I am utterly convinced it's more than that....

I'll tell you though we went into last Christmas (2016) with just three days of work booked in and I lost no sleep over it, 'something' would drop in, and it did, on the first day back, two weeks work dropped in for the beginning of February, the next day, the two weeks before it and then the next day the next week went too which just left one week to fill and that went the week after. Three days to six weeks. We had the best January ever, possibly the best month ever and I had 70% of the money to pay for the wedding and the honeymoon. Does the law of attraction work, Oh YES!

I still sometimes wake up in the middle of the night if there is something bothering me, but I don't have that stomach wrenching feeling of anxiety anymore and I have strategies to slow my mind down. It's amazing how productive the brain can actually be at this time of night though, some of my best ideas and solutions have come at this time. So if you wake up with an over active mind, don't fight it, embrace it!

And it looks like the music thing is about to come together, been discussing a project with Deb and we are going see where that goes once I've got the book out into other people's sphere's!

So, the three year pond, do you get it? There's certainly a lot of absurdities.

You see as well as understanding and knowing how to put your mind at peace, I believe you need to put your body in the best surroundings for you. And as we come from nature, connecting with that power is also vital.

So 'how to be happy according to Simon'. It really is take responsibility for everything you do, and I do mean everything. How you deal with yourself, how you deal with those around you, on a personal and a professional level. On a physical and spiritual level, and have faith in yourself. Have a plan for what you want, but look after now. If you've got all this right, you won't have to worry about tomorrow.

And the rest, well I have plans for world domination and this is just one step of that voyage, as I said, I'm not there yet by any means, but the rest of that is just another story, see you next time...